Quakers and their Meeting Houses

Quakers and their Meeting Houses

Chris Skidmore

 Historic England

Published by Liverpool University Press on behalf of Historic England,
The Engine House, Fire Fly Avenue, Swindon SN2 2EH
www.HistoricEngland.org.uk

Historic England is a Government service championing England's heritage and
giving expert, constructive advice.

The views contained in this book are those of the author alone and not
Historic England or Liverpool University Press.

First published 2021

ISBN: 978-1-80085-720-9 hardback
eISBN: 978-1-80207-080-4

British Library Cataloguing in Publication data
A CIP catalogue record for this book is available from the British Library.

Chris Skidmore has asserted the right to be identified as the author of this book in
accordance with the Copyright, Designs and Patents Act 1988.

Typeset in Charter 9/11

Page layout by Carnegie Book Production

Printed by Gomer.

Front cover: Brigflatts meeting house

Back cover: Farfield meeting house

Contents

Foreword

Quakers and their Meeting Houses is an informative and insightful account of the buildings that serve the Religious Society of Friends (Quakers), and is the culmination of the Religious Society of Friends and Historic England's joint Quaker Meeting Houses Heritage Project. The aim was to discover more about the Quaker built heritage through a combination of local and national expertise. In line with Quaker values and practice, meeting houses are not flamboyant or attention-seeking places, but they are nevertheless significant: even the most modest of meeting houses shows respect for the materials used and the craftsmen who shaped them. They speak of thoughtful design alongside functionality and simplicity, being creative spaces that energise action and witness within and beyond the Quaker meeting. All those involved in the project have been inspired by what has been discovered and have been touched by the lives of those of whom these buildings speak.

The Religious Society of Friends and Historic England have much enjoyed, and benefited from, working together, a process greatly facilitated by the helpfulness and hospitality of the current custodians of the meeting houses. In reading Chris Skidmore's careful account of the history behind Quaker architecture, we hope you too will find a new appreciation of Quaker heritage.

Sir Laurie Magnus
Chairman, Historic England

Paul Parker
Recording clerk, Britain Yearly Meeting

Preface

This book aims to give an account of the architecture and historical development of the Quaker meeting house, a distinctive building type, used as a place of worship by members of the Society of Friends (Quakers). It also attempts to map how the changing beliefs and practices of Quakers over the last 350 years have affected the architecture of the meeting house. Because Quakerism arose in England and, until the late 19th century, remained substantially restricted to the English-speaking world, the geographical focus of the buildings discussed is largely restricted to British examples. Nevertheless, since Quakerism spread rapidly to the transatlantic colonies and some unity of practice was maintained by visitation between England and America, there is some discussion of surviving American meeting houses of the colonial period.

The genesis of this book lay in the Quaker Meeting Houses Heritage Project, a national survey of Quaker meeting houses carried out between 2014 and 2016 by the Architectural History Practice Ltd (AHP). It was joint funded by Historic England (HE; formerly English Heritage) and Quakers in Britain[1] and was part of a wider HE project called 'Taking Stock', which aimed to assess the heritage significance of places of worship. The geographic extent was eventually extended beyond HE boundaries to include the Channel Islands, Scotland and Wales. Irish meeting houses were not covered since there is a separate Quaker organisation for the whole island of Ireland.

Three hundred and forty-five meeting houses were visited and reports written detailing their history and architecture as well as their accessibility, sustainability and use in the community. This represented all the meeting houses currently owned by British Quakers, the rest of whose just over 450 worshipping groups meet in rented premises.

After the end of the project, I was invited to write a book to make public these results and to bring the Quaker meeting house to a wider audience, much as *A Glimpse of Heaven*[2] did for the Roman Catholic branch of 'Taking Stock'. The Heritage Project reports form a major source of information for the book. However, in taking a historical approach, I have also chosen to consider some of the many buildings which have served as Quaker meeting houses in the past and which have been adapted to other uses or demolished. I also pay some attention to other Quaker buildings and to the burial grounds which are associated with meeting houses.

This book is dedicated jointly to my father, David Skidmore, whose gift of a chapel upbringing started my interest in the Nonconformist heritage, and to Ted Milligan, doyen of 20th-century Quaker historians, who died during the writing of this book and who first encouraged me to research Quaker history.

Chris Skidmore
January 2021

Notes

1 'Quakers in Britain' is the short title used by the central organisation of British Quakers. It is properly referred to as the Yearly Meeting of the Religious Society of Friends (Quakers) in Britain or Britain Yearly Meeting. It comprises all the Quaker meetings in England, Scotland, Wales and the Channel Islands.

2 Martin 2009.

Acknowledgements

My thanks must go first to all those who were involved in the Quaker Meeting Houses Heritage Project, notably the staff of the AHP but also the volunteers from Quaker meetings up and down the country who helped source and collate the information involved. Many of them have also willingly welcomed me to their meeting houses or provided extra information and thereby earned my extra thanks.

In my wider research I owe an enormous debt to the late David Butler both for his friendship and for the research accumulated in his two-volume *The Quaker Meeting Houses of Britain* (1999), which contains information about the over 800 places in Britain for which there is evidence of a Quaker meeting.

To Ingrid Greenhow I owe the suggestion that I should write this book: it has been a gift that keeps on giving! She has, together with Lis Burch and Linda Monckton, supported me and offered useful comments on my writing. Chris Wakeling has, since we first met, encouraged me in writing about places of worship and has, with typical generosity, helped me to avoid most of the pitfalls that beset the tyro researcher in a new field. Any errors which persist remain mine and mine alone.

Thanks are also due to the staff at Liverpool University Press and Carnegie Book Production for guiding this cuckoo in their nest through publication, as if it had been their own.

I am most grateful to have been allowed access to a large number of images from the Historic England Archive. I am also greatly indebted to John Hall, whose Flickr albums at www.flickr.com/photos/qmh/ provide the most comprehensive photographic coverage of Quaker meeting houses available and from which I have used a substantial number of images. A number of individual photographers, both professional and amateur, have allowed me to use their images, and Quaker meeting houses have granted me permission to use images from their archives. I am grateful to them all for their cooperation.

The restrictions imposed by the coronavirus pandemic have prevented the production of new images from a number of archive items. In most cases I have been able to scan and use the images in copyright publications to replace these. I am sincerely grateful to the families of David Butler and Hubert Lidbetter for giving permission for the use of these images.

Finally, Gil Skidmore has been a constant and loving support to me both during the research for and the writing of this book. The understanding of the arc of Quaker history presented here is our joint one, developed over many years of argument and discussion, but set down finally in my words.

Fig 0.1
Fox's pulpit on Firbank Fell,
Cumbria. Said to be the
rock from which George Fox
preached to the Westmorland
Seekers at Whitsuntide 1652.
A graveyard stands nearby
which may mark the site of
the chapel of ease in which the
Seekers were meeting.

Introduction

The Society of Friends (Quakers) is a child of the 17th century. The story of the Quaker movement is rooted in the religious and political turmoil that accompanied the dispute between the Crown and Parliament which began in the 1630s, led to the civil wars of the 1640s and 1650s, and to the experiment of an English republic that characterised that latter decade. This part of the national story has been told countless times.

The religious background

The essence is that the events of the 16th century had resulted in improved educational opportunities, an increasingly literate population with little to read except English translations of the Bible, and an only partly reformed English Church. All had the possibility of observing for themselves the mismatch between the story of the early Church told in the gospels and the book of Acts and the institution which was the Church. The removal of central authority within the Church – the bishops and the ecclesiastical courts – during the Commonwealth, which also, of course, removed ecclesiastical censorship, led to a torrent of ideas which now could be readily disseminated by publication.

There was turmoil within the Church of England itself, not only over doctrine and liturgy, as a debate raged over Church government. On one side was the congregationalist idea that the gathered Church (the godly folk and their pastor) in a particular place was the ultimate authority and, on the other, ideas of hierarchical government by bishops (episcopacy) or priests (presbyterianism). Outside the Church there were also groups of dissenters, known as 'separates' (being separated from the national Church), meeting for worship. The most numerous of these were the Baptists, who highlighted adult baptism as necessary for the believer. Many independent churches had pastors who had themselves been priests in the Church of England: others were led by members of the congregation, often with social standing in their community. Important for the Quaker story are the Seekers, an amorphous collection of independent groups, who saw all churches as corrupt and awaited the receipt of the Spirit of Christ to show them the way forward. They shunned religious rituals and met in silence. Finally, this was also a time when those with a vision travelled the country as itinerant preachers or evangelists, attempting to spread their version of the gospel. They could preach in the open air, at public gatherings, such as fairs, or, if the pastor allowed it, in church after the sermon had been delivered.

During the Commonwealth period, all religious groups outside the national Church could be subject to prosecution for their views, either for non-attendance at the parish church, for disturbing church services, in extreme cases for blasphemy and, if they were itinerants, for vagrancy.

However, the New Model Army, which had won the war for Parliament and remained a force to be reckoned with throughout this period, consisted largely of those with dissenting views and provided a safe space for debate and heterodox opinions. Numbers of pastors and preachers became chaplains to various regiments and hence gained extra support. A number of early Quaker leaders had held positions and undergone formative experiences in the army.

Early Quaker evangelism

George Fox (1624–91) came to be seen as the leading light among the Quaker evangelists of the 1650s when the movement first came to prominence. In truth there were a number of important evangelists, including Elizabeth Hooton, James Nayler, Richard Farnsworth, Francis Howgill, Edward Burrough, Richard Hubberthorne and William Edmondson. From a modern perspective, Fox's prominence was at least in part due to his robust constitution, which allowed him to survive long and multiple imprisonments, to his relative longevity, and to the posthumous publication of his *Journal* in 1694, with its vivid account of his part in the rise of the movement.

Starting in about 1645 in his native Midlands, Fox's preaching drew together men and women, largely from already separated congregations, with his message that 'Christ has come to teach his People himself'. The group was at this time known as 'The Children of the Light'. Fox was a charismatic preacher and often trembled 'in the power of the Lord' as he spoke, a characteristic which led to the nickname, bestowed on the group by a Derby justice, of 'Quakers'. Around 1652, having attracted further converts from the Doncaster area, members of the group began to evangelise the north of England. Fox himself headed towards the Pennines and on Firbank Fell, between Kendal and Sedbergh, at Whitsuntide 1652, met with, preached to and converted a large gathering of Seekers, who met in a neighbouring chapel of ease (Fig 0.1). Fox had become their prophet, showing them how to receive the Spirit of Christ that they sought.

Venturing westward into Lancashire, Fox was invited to stay at Swarthmoor Hall near Ulverston (Fig 0.2). Its owner was Thomas Fell, a Judge of Assize and Member of Parliament, whose house was open to those travelling with a message. However, it was his wife, Margaret (born Askew, 1614–1702), who became a Quaker convert and turned her home into the powerhouse of the Quaker movement, acting as chief administrator, fundraiser and as a focus for the voluminous correspondence that held together what became a national movement. She was a strong supporter of Fox's leadership and, Thomas Fell having died in 1658, she and Fox were subsequently married in 1669.

From the 1652 meeting of Fox and the Westmorland Seekers came a crusade to evangelise the whole country by a further 50 or more converts, travelling often in pairs, so that by the end of 1654 there was a Quaker presence in most parts of England and also in Ireland (Wales and Scotland proved much less receptive). At the height of this missionary activity there were perhaps some 50,000 to 60,000 Quakers out of a population of

Fig 0.2
Swarthmoor Hall, Ulverston.
In this late 16th-century
house lived Judge Thomas
Fell, his wife Margaret and
their family. George Fox
visited here in 1652 and it
subsequently became the
centre of Quaker missionary
activity across the country.
The building was owned
by the Fells and their
descendants the Abrahams
until 1759 and then passed
out of the family until
Emma Clarke Abraham, a
descendant, was helped to buy
it in 1912. She refurbished
the Hall and it was eventually
bought by British Quakers
in 1954. The Grade II* listed
building is open to the public
and has been adapted for use
as visitor accommodation and
as a conference centre.

5 million. Such was the success of the mission to London that the Quakers involved found it necessary to hire for their meetings a room in the Bull and Mouth inn in St-Martin-le-Grand that would hold 1,000 people.

Quaker missionaries had some success in Holland and Germany and also reached the transatlantic colonies, arriving in New England in 1656, New York, Maryland, Virginia and the Carolinas in 1657, and Barbados and Jamaica in 1661. East and West Jersey were founded as Quaker colonies in 1674 and 1681 respectively, Pennsylvania following in the next two years.

The Quaker message

What characterised the Quaker message at this stage was
- that there is 'that of God' in everyone;
- that this 'Inner Light' will act as a teacher and guide and inspire prophesy;
- that neither clergy nor consecrated buildings are necessary;
- that it is the spiritual experience behind scripture not scripture itself that is God-given;
- that a life lived in the Light can return one to the innocence of Adam and Eve in Paradise;
- that actions performed in the Light can bring about Christ's kingdom on earth.

The radical version of equality implied by the first of these points led Quakers to act socially as equals to all, using the second person singular 'thou' to everybody rather than just to close family and neglecting deferential behaviour, such as removing one's hat in the presence of social superiors. It also led to insistence on fair and just behaviour in social interactions, in commerce and in the justice system.

The second point called for right living and in particular the use of the truth at all times. This led to a refusal to qualify some statements as more true than others by the use of oaths, a position supported by scripture. The third led to a refusal to pay taxes – tithes – to support the national Church and to an urgent requirement to find alternatives to burial in a churchyard, over which parish clergy had a monopoly. These issues caused further social friction.

However, it was the last three points on which critics often focused because they challenged the theological bases even of dissenting theology, questioning the primacy of scripture, the ideas of original sin, and of Calvinist notions of election, as well as suggesting that it should be good works not faith which is the mark of the true Christian. They also led to Quakers being accused of antinomianism (of believing that the saved were freed from the constraints of the law and society) like the Ranters, and being confused with apocalyptic sects like the Fifth Monarchists (who wanted to bring about Christ's coming by force), and even with the Jesuits.

Quaker meetings

Quakers held three sorts of religious meeting. The first was a meeting for the purpose of preaching and evangelisation, bringing non-Quakers to a realisation of and identification with the Quaker message. These threshing meetings – for the public was being 'threshed' to distinguish the potential converts from the rest – were generally held in public spaces, in churchyards, marketplaces, inn yards and in the open air, as George Fox did in 1652 on Firbank Fell. This was the chief means of those Quakers who first evangelised Britain in 1652 to 1655. Meetings of this kind continued to be held by travelling Quaker preachers, both men and women, throughout the 18th century. There was no particular need to have a specific building for this purpose and, indeed, the spontaneous nature of such meetings – preachers were expected to wait upon the movement of the spirit before holding them – meant that the place was likely to be the best that could be obtained in the time. In early times open-air spaces were favoured; later ages used rooms in inns, assembly halls, even tennis courts: temporary structures called booths were sometimes built for this purpose (*see* pages 55–6).

The second meeting was the meeting for worship, held on a regular basis, which was about nurturing those converts and building them, along with existing Quakers, into a supportive worshipping community which inspired them to live better lives and enabled them to seek to change the world. Meetings for worship took a form, derived from Seeker practice, of silent waiting for a message to be given to and shared by a member of the meeting with time left between contributions (known as 'ministry') for reflection on what had been offered. Meetings for worship continue in this form to the present day: they are not deliberately silent but can and do proceed without ministry.

The third meeting was a development of the second, for Quakers carried out the business of the group within a meeting for worship. These business meetings were held separately and less frequently than the regular meeting for worship, with a clerk sitting at a table, preparing the minutes of business taken and submitting them to the members present for agreement. The clerk, who acted as both chair and secretary, also presented the matters for consideration. All members could contribute to the meeting, but were expected to use the same discernment as they might in a regular meeting for worship before speaking – spoken contributions were similarly considered as ministry. The intention was to discover not consensus but what was the right way forward (described by some as the 'will of God') for the group. This way of proceeding with business has come to be known as the 'Quaker business method' and continues to be the pattern within the Society of Friends today.

Men, women and children all attended meetings for worship; however, men and women were given distinct areas of influence in regard to business and so separate business meetings were held for the two sexes.

Penalties and persecution

The rapid spread of Quakerism as a coherent and apparently well-organised movement, where constant communication between members and groups was encouraged, made Quakers a focus of suspicion, particularly in the uncertain times of the 1650s. Although Fox and other leaders had cordial relations with some of the Parliamentarian leaders, including Cromwell, Ireton and Lambert, local magistrates were often not well disposed to a body which seemed bent on upsetting the social order. Prosecutions for disturbing worship and for blasphemy often attracted heavy sentences and even calls for capital punishment, and a number of Quaker leaders, including Fox himself, spent many years in prison. Given the unsavoury state of 17th-century gaols, long incarceration could itself be a death sentence.

The most severe treatment was visited on the charismatic Quaker preacher, James Nayler, when his attempt to act out Jesus' entry into Jerusalem (at Bristol in 1656) became a national scandal. After trial before Parliament he was sentenced to be whipped, pilloried, branded and imprisoned. Persecution was even harsher across the Atlantic in the Puritan Massachusetts Bay Colony, where Marmaduke Stevenson and William Robinson were hanged in 1659, as were Mary Dyer and William Leddra the following year.

However, it was not until the restoration of the monarchy in the person of Charles II in 1660 that persecution of Quakers, along with other dissenters, became embedded in statute law. Although Charles had promised religious toleration in the Declaration of Breda before his return, he found himself unable to carry it out in the face of the Cavalier Parliament, which wished to bring back the religious *status quo ante*. Following the Fifth Monarchist rising in January 1661, which brought forth from George Fox and other Quakers the first public statement of Friends' determination to avoid armed conflict (the so-called 'peace testimony'), the Parliament also had a political excuse for treating dissenters as revolutionaries. A series of Acts known as the Clarendon Code[1] were passed over the next few years which effectively made dissenting worship illegal and turned dissenters into second-class citizens. In particular, the Quaker Act of 1662 made it illegal to 'wilfully and obstinately refuse' to take a legal oath and also for Quakers to 'assemble themselves to the number of five or more of the age of sixteen yeares or upwards at any one time in any place under pretence of joyning in a Religious Worship'. The penalty was a £5 fine and three months imprisonment for a first offence, rising on a third offence to liability to transportation for life.

Although Quakers were not alone in suffering imprisonment under the Clarendon Code, they were the most severely treated group. This was partly because they refused to conceal their meetings for worship, often worshipping while in prison and returning to regular worship immediately upon being released. However, magistrates did not always find it easy to convict Quakers, as witnesses could often say no more than that they observed folk sitting together in silence, and juries were often reluctant to act against peaceable neighbours.

It was Quakers' refusal to swear oaths that brought the worst treatment because it laid them open to the legal pitfall that was the oath of allegiance. This had been introduced originally as an anti-Catholic measure, for it included an abjuration of papal authority, but it served equally well to trap the Quakers. A failure to take the oath allowed you to be represented as disloyal and potentially traitorous. The authorities no longer needed to obtain convictions under the Clarendon Code but could simply administer the oath for which the penalty for first refusal was itself imprisonment. Failure to swear a second time could then be used to invoke the ancient statute of *praemunire*, which led to forfeiture of property and imprisonment for life or at the king's pleasure.

Quaker organisation

As the millenarian enthusiasm of the early period began to die down and the problems of maintaining the Quaker movement for the future became clearer, Fox, among others, persuaded Friends to adopt a national structure and some limit on spiritual liberty. Although each Quaker had access to their inner teacher, it was clear that not all were equally practised at interpreting the spiritual leadings they received and distinguishing between their individual self-will and what was the right thing for the group. The solution was that all leadings of the spirit were to be submitted to the local business meeting for discernment.

If matters were of wider significance, they should then be submitted to the consideration of a wider body. Fox worked hard, beginning in the penal period, to build a nationwide structure of meetings, starting with the local worshipping group, supported and monitored by bodies (meetings) at district level, meeting monthly; at county level, meeting quarterly; and at national level, meeting yearly. Here the use of 'meeting' not only refers to the gathering itself but also to the Quakers who comprise it, in a somewhat analogous way to the use of 'church' to mean both the building and the congregation which worships in it.

These monthly, quarterly and yearly meetings, along with the advice that they disseminated, were together referred to by Fox as 'gospel order'. Decisions taken by these meetings were considered binding on all Quakers making up that level of the structure. This structure not only nurtured the growth of the movement but acted as a source of spiritual authority to discourage the individualistic and antinomian tendencies which were inevitably attendant on the theology of the 'Inner Light'.

Growth and toleration

Despite the fact that some 15,000 Quakers were imprisoned during Charles II's reign and some 450 died as a result, persecution, as is often the case, proved ineffective. In fact, it may even have had the opposite effect: the presbyterian Richard Baxter thought that 'many turned Quakers, because the Quakers kept their meetings openly and went to prison for it cheerfully'.[2] What effects it had were also uneven, both geographically and through time, depending as they did on the willingness of local magistrates to apply the full strictures of the law. The Quaker groups founded by the evangelists of the 1650s and supported by the structure introduced during the 1670s and 1680s continued to grow.

The brief reign of James II saw a suspension of the penal laws. They were not to return, as the triumph of William and Mary led to the passing of the Toleration Act of 1689 which allowed trinitarian dissenters to worship freely while retaining the penal laws against Catholics. Worship had to be conducted openly and not behind closed doors and meeting houses had to be registered with the magistrates. Nevertheless, all dissenters suffered from the continuing effects of the Corporation Act and the Test Acts of the 1670s, which excluded them from public office. They were also barred from the English universities, which operated religious tests. Quakers, in particular, were also liable to restraint of goods and even imprisonment if they refused to pay tithes.

At this point there were in England and Wales perhaps some 700 Quaker worshipping groups under the umbrella of London Yearly Meeting, which has met annually since about 1668. Quaker evangelism had also been successful in the expanding American colonies both in the Caribbean, particularly in Jamaica and Barbados, and along the eastern seaboard of the mainland. Yearly Meetings were founded in Rhode Island in 1661, Baltimore in 1672, Philadelphia in 1681 and New York in 1696.

All these Quakers needed buildings in which to meet and worship and it is to this subject that we turn in the following chapters.

Notes

1   These were the Corporation Act (1661), which restricted membership of town corporations to Anglican communicants; the Act of Uniformity (1662), which removed priests with dissenting views from the Church of England; the Quaker Act (1662); the Conventicle Act (1664), which extended the Quaker Act to other dissenters; and the Five Mile Act (1665), which banned former priests from the areas in which they had ministered. The Conventicle Act was renewed in 1670 with financial rewards for informants. The first Test Act of 1673 extended the ban on dissenters to civil and military office.

2   Reliquiae Baxterianae, part ii, 437 (as quoted in Watts 1978, 245).

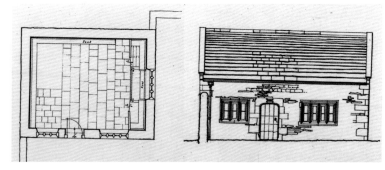

Fig 1.1
Farfield meeting house – plan
and elevation.
[Drawings by H Godwin
Arnold]

Fig 1.2
Farfield meeting house from
the east. Note the early
gravestones against the gable
wall.

Fig 1.3
The interior of Farfield
meeting house, showing the
ministers' stand.

1 Buildings of utmost simplicity

Early meeting houses to 1715: Part 1

The requirements of a building for regular meetings for worship are few. Without priests or pastors nor the formal requirements of a liturgy, Quaker meeting houses seem to be the essence of simplicity.

In the beginning, Quakers often met wherever was most convenient, whether in the house of one or other member of the local congregation or in a convenient structure, such as a barn. Outdoor meetings for worship were also not unknown. At Pardshaw, in the north of Cumberland, Quakers met during the summer 'without Doors, for many years, on a place called Pardshow Cragg'[1] and divided for worship into four houses at different locations for the necessary warmth during the winter months. This arrangement continued for nearly 20 years until in 1672 they built their first meeting house. Some burial grounds were also used as meeting places, as at Colthouse in Cumbria, where there are stone flags projecting from the wall which could be used as seats (first mentioned in 1669).

Meeting houses carried with them the risk, during the penal period, that they could be targeted by the authorities, furniture could be removed or the premises sealed up or even sometimes demolished. Soon after the passing of the Conventicle Act in 1670, the King's Council ordered the demolition of the meeting house at Horsleydown in Southwark, and three months later, that at Ratcliff in Stepney was also demolished, but such radical action was rare outside the larger towns and cities.

Worshipping outdoors removed the possibility that a building could be demolished and its owner or tenant prosecuted. However, the public nature of the meeting for worship was seen as an important witness to the truth of the Quaker message: meeting outdoors in remote places, as the Covenanters did in Scotland, was deplored, and Friends were exhorted not to 'decline, forsake, or remove their public assemblies, because of times of suffering' or 'because of informers and the like persecutors'.[2]

Despite the restrictions on dissenting worship imposed by the Clarendon Code, it is remarkable that more than 200 meeting houses were opened for worship between 1660 and 1689; some 18 of these survive, although modified in part over the subsequent centuries. These survivors present a diverse group of buildings with few external stylistic similarities. From what we know, about half of these used existing buildings and about half were built for their purpose. Local groups of Quakers built where they could purchase or be gifted suitable land, largely using their own labour and thus, perhaps unsurprisingly, adopted the vernacular style of the buildings around them.

Farfield and Ettington

Despite the lack of external similarities, early Quaker meeting houses do indeed share some characteristic architectural features. We can see these most readily at the preserved meeting house at Farfield, near Addingham, in Wharfedale, built in 1689 by Anthony Myers, the owner of nearby Farfield Hall. Because of its relatively remote location and its abandonment as a place for regular worship after a little over 100 years, it retains many of its original features.

Figures 1.1 and 1.2 show what appears to be a typical cottage design for late 17th-century Yorkshire: a rectangular single-celled building of three bays with a central door, built of the local stone with a stone slated roof and a stone flagged floor. Two mullioned windows sit either side of the door and there is a third window set higher in the east wall. Ashlar blocks have been used for the quoins and the door surround, and the walls are rubble.

The meeting house is set at one side of a larger plot which had been given to Friends over 20 years before as a burial ground, a situation not uncommon at the time. There was then no provision for burial except in the parish churchyard and Quakers, wherever possible, rejected it as a place for interment. This led to the provision of separate burial grounds as a pressing issue from the earliest days. The majority of these early burial grounds are distinctive in that they contain no monuments: Friends witnessed to the equality of all by limiting the cost of burial to what all could afford (formalised by Yearly Meeting minutes in 1717 and 1766). Farfield, however, is an exception, since it retains several early gravestones and a striking block of family chest tombs.

There are two elements of fixed furniture shown on the plan, which are seen more clearly in the picture of the interior in Fig 1.3. These are simple fixed benches round the west and north walls and a more complex structure on the east wall, which is known as the ministers' stand. It comprises a raised bench with a panelled surround, the central section of which is raised up a further step and is fronted by a balustraded rail. The ministers' stand was a feature of all Quaker meeting houses until the late 19th century. It provides a focus for the other loose benches which are arranged facing it.

The origins of the ministers' stand are obscure. As a piece of furniture, it most resembles the bench in a manorial court of the period,[3] except that it has no known association with judgement. It was here originally, we think, that the most spiritually respected Quakers – what were referred to as 'antient Friends' – sat: this distinction was formalised in the early 18th century by appointing Friends, known as elders, who were responsible for the conduct of the meeting for worship. It also became clear from early on that there were some Quakers who were skilled in ministry, that is, in speaking in the meeting for worship, and they too began formally to be appointed by their meetings as 'ministers'. Because of their need to be heard, ministers would sit on the raised benches alongside the elders; where there were two or more levels in a stand, the ministers sat at the higher level and hence the structure became known as the ministers' stand. It is functionally equivalent to the pulpit in a chapel, without showing any structural similarities.

Fig 1.4
Skipton meeting house, built 1693.

Fig 1.5
Rawdon meeting house, built 1697, the right-hand bay added in 1729.

Fig 1.6
Askwith meeting house, built 1705 and closed by 1800 – converted to a dwelling in 1981.

Fig 1.7
Ettington meeting house, built
1684; the extension on the left
built 1986.

Fig 1.8
Ettington interior, showing
the short stand and the rush
matting dado.

Seating within a meeting house is thought to have been initially on crude forms, barely more than a plank with occasional vertical supports, as would have been common in the 17th century in many public places. Through time these progressed to benches by the addition of backs. When extra comfort became desirable, vertical supports were raked backwards and extra width added to seats at the front; these changes can be observed in surviving meeting-house benches. The use of bought-in pews – as in other denominations – was something that did not develop until well into the 19th century. Benches and pews were rarely if ever fixed to the floor.

In the same area of the former West Riding as Farfield there are three other meeting houses of a broadly similar design, cottage-like and of two or three bays with the entrance in the long wall (Figs 1.4–1.6): they are Skipton (1693), Rawdon (1697) and Askwith (1705, and now a private residence). They demonstrate the influence of the regional vernacular over their design.

A similar small rural meeting house is still in use at Ettington, Warwickshire, near Stratford-upon-Avon (Fig 1.7). The land on which the meeting house stands was given to Quakers in 1681 and the meeting house built from 1684: it was registered following the Act of Toleration in 1689. It is built of coursed limestone rubble with ironstone quoins and ashlar dressings; it originally had a roof of stone flags, but these were replaced by slate in 1894. As originally built, it had no window in the south-east gable end: the two windows beyond the door on the south-west-facing long wall are of three lights mullioned with their original leaded oblong panes. At one end of the building there is a small L-shaped extension containing a kitchen, toilet and a classroom built in 1986.

As at Farfield, the floor is flagged and the meeting room was open to the roof – a ceiling was added as late as 1942. There is a fixed bench here around all four walls (the current one a 19th-century replacement) with at one end a central raised two-tier stand. Above the fixed bench there is, unlike at Farfield, a dado, which may originally have been of wood but is now, remarkably, made of rush matting matched by rush bench mats (Fig 1.8).

The meeting houses at Farfield and Ettington show that simple cottage-like characteristics are relatively common in early structures and are not geographically restricted. Ettington demonstrates how the general form of a meeting house can survive intact but accommodate change over the passage of 300 years as the needs of the community change.

The use of dwelling houses

Early meeting houses were not always newly built. That at Portishead in North Somerset (Fig 1.9), which has been in use since 1670, is thought to have been adapted from an existing cottage. Again, it is largely rubble built but whitewashed and with a thatched roof, as fits the local vernacular. Originally it would have been a structure of three bays with a central doorway in the long wall between two windows, each of three leaded lights, one of which survives. At some point the entrance was moved to the gable end where it is now obscured by a porch. Other later changes conspire to obscure the three-bay form. Inside, there is a single undivided room with a stand, somewhat similar to that at Farfield, with a central raised bench and lower benches at either side.

At Broad Campden in the Cotswolds, a cottage of two bays, probably of the 16th century, was adapted as a meeting house in 1663, but was quickly extended by raising the roof and adding an extra bay, now containing the entrance door, in 1677 (Fig 1.10). It is built of coursed and squared rubblestone with a Cotswold stone tile roof and is lit by two four-light mullioned windows. The building has had a chequered history, like many meeting houses, with a period of closure from 1874 and let for a variety of purposes until, in 1961, the half-derelict building was bought back by local Quakers and restored. At that point the ministers' stand and the surrounding panelling were the only internal structures that survived. The present gallery and entrance lobby, screened from the meeting room, are therefore largely conjectural.

Fig 1.9 (above left)
Portishead meeting house, given in 1669.

Fig 1.10 (above right)
Broad Campden meeting house, bought in 1663.

Fig 1.11 (right)
St Helens meeting house, acquired in 1678.

A much larger house has been used as the Quaker meeting house in St Helens, Merseyside, since 1679 (Fig 1.11). It is now the oldest surviving building in the town, since the neighbouring chapel of St Helen, from which the town takes its name, burnt down in 1916. It was built in the late 16th or early 17th century and, as the frontage shows, was originally of two storeys with mullioned windows of up to six lights in both storeys, some of which retain diamond-leaded glazing. The large chimney stack to the left originally served a large fireplace and bread oven, evidencing the domestic origins of the building: these are now bricked up and concealed behind the 18th-century ministers' stand. The meeting room itself is now a five-bay double-height single-volume space.

The external appearance of the building also shows signs of updating. There has been a sundial, not unknown on Quaker buildings, associated with the building since 1691, although the current one above the door is dated to 1753. The roof appears to be of 19th-century origin, as are the two square metal ventilators on the roof ridge.

The variety of early meeting houses

Three meeting houses survive from 1672, when for one year Charles II suspended the laws against dissenters: one of these is at Alton in Hampshire (Fig 1.12).[4] The building is of two storeys and was built with a cottage at its north end under the same roof, subsequently incorporated into the meeting house. At the south end of the site there is a cross wing extending towards the road to give an L shape. The building is of brick, with the main elevation stuccoed; the hipped main roof is covered with hand-made clay tiles and the cross wing has a tile-hung first floor. To the north of the site a subsequent attached cottage of 1832 still serves as a separate dwelling. The whole, being in the local vernacular, fits well into the townscape on the main road leading north out of the town and within sight of the parish church: it is certainly not hiding away.

Fig 1.12
Alton meeting house, built 1672, from the south.

Fig 1.13
Alton interior, showing the former gallery and shutters at the south end of the meeting room.

The inclusion of a cottage in the same building as the meeting house, or on an adjacent site, is common for Quaker meeting houses. Such structures provide accommodation for resident wardens in modern times. In the 17th century there could be another reason for this provision, as it meant that the building could be classified as a dwelling and was therefore protected under common law from demolition. In the absence of a separate cottage, some Quaker meetings allowed one of their poorer members to live in the meeting house itself. This form of practical support outlived the period of persecution and more often than not involved the use of a separated part of the meeting house rather than the meeting room itself.

As can be imagined, the dual use of premises could lead to friction between the meeting and the tenant as in 1692 at Winchmore Hill in north London where the meeting minuted that 'widow French is to be acquainted that Friends are troubled to see that she does not put things out of sight during the meeting time as her pots and things upon the shelves and cheeses on the beams which are for all to see'.[5]

The interior of the Alton Meeting House has been changed several times since 1672. The large sash windows which now light the full-height meeting room date to 1735. The structure which dominates the south end of the room (Fig 1.13) is a screen comprising moveable shutters which conceals the balustraded upper gallery, built in 1690 to allow for the seating of an increasing number of worshippers. Underneath the gallery is a downstairs lobby; the shutters at the lower level are hinged so that they too can be folded away and thus increase the size of the meeting room.

This arrangement of a screen with moveable shutters to divide up the space in a meeting room is found in many Quaker meeting houses from the 17th to the 19th century, although the nature of the mechanism used to remove the shutters evolved over the centuries. In this early period the shutters could either be physically moved to one side or hinged, as here, so that the panels move aside like folding doors, or at the top, so the panels can be lifted up and secured to a hook on the ceiling. As well as separating a lobby or a gallery from the main room, shutters could also be used to create two meeting rooms side by side, so that men's and women's meetings for business could take place at the same time and place.

In the same year, 1672, in the remote Herefordshire village of Almeley Wootton, Roger Prichard 'built a meeting house upon his land, at his own charge, and gave it freely to friends'.[6] Edward Prichard, son of Roger, was one of the 13 signatories of William Penn's 1682 Charter for Pennsylvania, and with his brother-in-law, William Eckley, was one of the first purchasers of land in the province. This gives the meeting house extra historical resonance.

The meeting house is a timber-framed structure of two bays with square panels, infilled with plaster, on a sandstone plinth with a half-hipped roof of clay tiles. Externally the wall panels are painted white, giving the distinctive checkerboard appearance of the Herefordshire vernacular. The gable end away from the road is horizontally boarded; the original door is protected by a porch/lobby. The current state of these latter elements, together with all the windows, are the result of a major restoration in 1955–6 (Fig 1.14).

Fig 1.14
Almeley Wootton meeting house, built 1672, from the burial ground, showing the porch.

Fig 1.15
Almeley Wootton meeting house from the south, showing the gallery windows, the roof and chimney stack.

From the south the building appears to be a two-storey structure (Fig 1.15) with a large external stone chimney stack, as at St Helens serving a bread oven. This is probably not original but dates to the period between 1797 and 1891 when the building was not used for worship but in part as a dwelling house.

Inside, the meeting house is open to the rafters and for half of its length is divided vertically by a balustraded gallery, reached by an open stairway consisting of two flights with a half-landing. The gallery may originally have had shutters. No fitted furnishings survive and the loose benches date from the 19th century.

Even more closely associated with William Penn is the meeting house at Coolham, near Horsham in Sussex, which is known as the Blue Idol. Penn lived at nearby Warminghurst between 1677 and 1696 and was involved with other local Friends in trying to establish a meeting and find a place to meet. In the early 1690s the group purchased for £20 a late 16th-century farmhouse and some land from a local farmer, which they adapted as a meeting house. The original two-storey building, seen in Fig 1.16, is timber framed with plaster in-filling on a brick base with a roof of Horsham stone slabs. There is a large window into the full-height meeting room. The end wall is weather boarded and contains the entrance door to the meeting room with a window above and another dormer window in the roof.

The Blue Idol has had a varied history of neglect, restoration and extension. The meeting house closed in 1791, reopening in 1874 for worship which has continued to the present day. The rest of the farmhouse has been used at times as a caretaker's house. This part of the structure has been extended three times: first in 1893, then in 1934–5 by Hubert Lidbetter, and again in 1969. It was in use for about 80 years as a guest house but is now again a private dwelling.

About 20 miles to the north-east, at Ifield in Sussex, now incorporated into Crawley New Town, is another early meeting house attached to a much earlier house, in this case a hall house of *c* 1475, known as 'The Old Forge'. This was bought from the Quaker blacksmith

Fig 1.16
Coolham meeting house –
the Blue Idol – adapted for
worship 1692. The section
containing the meeting room
is in the foreground.

Robert Robinson in 1674 and the meeting house built alongside in the next two years. The building is of squared Sussex stone with a complex Horsham stone roof. There is a central door in the long wall, the lintel inscribed 1676, and above this to either side two half-hipped gables (Fig 1.17). There are leaded three-light windows either side of the entrance with timber transoms.

Inside, the space is divided into two by a full-height timber screen with double sash shutters built in 1822. The right-hand space is the current meeting room with a ministers' bench stretching the length of one wall, dado panelling, timber floors and loose benches. It is dominated by a single timber post with braces which supports the ceiling and, presumably, the roof. The left-hand space was formerly the women's meeting room and now makes a cosy library.

Another meeting house that, like Farfield and Almeley Wootton, owes its foundation to a wealthy local landowner is that at Adderbury, south of Banbury in Oxfordshire, which was built in 1675 by Bray Doyley, lord of the manor of West Adderbury, who was soon afterwards

Fig 1.17
Ifield meeting house, built
1676. Robert Robinson's
house is on the left. A brick
mounting block stands by the
path.

Fig 1.18
Adderbury meeting house, built 1675.

Fig 1.19
Adderbury interior. [Watercolour by Mary Baker c 1885]

imprisoned for two months for allowing its construction. It is built in coursed squared blocks of the local reddish marlstone and has a steep-pitched roof (Fig 1.18). There is a gable-end chimney stack, which has been rebuilt at some point and carries a renewed datestone. The front is symmetrical with a central double doorway and two large three-light windows; above the door is a gabled dormer with a two-light casement window.

Although apparently a single-storey building, the interior is divided vertically by a balustraded gallery around three sides (Fig 1.19). Below, the floor is flagged and the walls have tongue-and-grooved panelling to dado height. The raised ministers' stand extends along the north wall, opposite the door, and has a central raised section and an elders' bench in front. It is of 18th-century design. There is a fireplace in the north-east corner. Both gable ends have windows which serve to light the gallery.

In the later 17th century, cottages were built opposite the meeting house, one of which became the space for the women's business meeting. Butler conjectures that this led to a reordering of the meeting house layout from the more usual arrangement of ministers' stand on the gable wall facing a gallery above half the floor area (the women meeting upstairs) – as found at Alton and Almeley Wootton – to the more unusual one found here.[7]

Brigflatts and other early Cumbrian meeting houses

One of the best known of early Quaker meeting houses is at Brigflatts, near Sedbergh in Cumbria. This hamlet, founded by flax weavers on the river Rawthey, was one of the first places visited by George Fox in 1652 when he stayed at the house of Richard Robinson. Fox founded the meeting here in the same year, but it was not until 1675 that a meeting house was built on land formerly owned by Richard Robinson and bought for 10 shillings the previous year. As was often the case, the materials were transported to the site and the building erected by Quakers themselves.

The external appearance of the building is very much that of a substantial local farmhouse of the period (Fig 1.20). It is constructed of lime-washed random rubble with a roof of stone slates. The two-storey structure is of four bays with the second bay occupied by a two-storey

Fig 1.20
Brigflatts meeting house,
built 1675.

Fig 1.21
Brigflatts, interior with
stand on the left and original
gallery straight ahead.

Fig 1.22
Stable and schoolroom at
Brigflatts.

porch. The outer bays each contain a pair of two-light mullioned windows to ground and first floors and in the third bay two three-light mullioned windows light the full-height meeting room.

The porch is a distinctive feature, being almost like that of a church. It has a round-arched outer open doorway with chamfered stone surround. Above the doorway is a replica of the original datestone and a small round-headed window, lighting an upper room. There is no outer door: it has a stone floor, stone benches to either side, and a square-headed inner doorway. The studded oak door of 1706 leads via an internal draught lobby to the main meeting room.

The ministers' stand, raised on three steps above an elders' bench, is situated on the long outer wall underneath the two three-light windows, just as the pulpit might be in a long-wall meeting house of the period (on the left in Fig 1.21). There are fixed benches around the meeting room and dado panelling lines the walls. Originally the roof was open to the rafters and the meeting minutes show that every year Friends were appointed to stuff moss into the gaps between the roof flags to reduce the draught.

Many of the changes that brought about the present arrangement of the meeting house were carried out within the building's first 50 years. To replace the original earth floor a wooden floor was added in 1681 (since replaced several times) and a plaster ceiling was constructed in 1711. There was originally a gallery at one end of the room, in the first bay and reached by a ladder: the L-shaped gallery on rounded wooden columns was added by 1714. This required a wider staircase, at the bottom of which was the 'dog pen' for the convenience of the owners of working dogs. It was only in 1749 that a partition with shutters was added to the original gallery to separate a room for the women's business meeting. Around 1900 the first bay of the building was extensively remodelled to create a caretaker's cottage, which has since been superseded by the purchase of Rosebank, the 19th-century villa which lies behind the meeting house.

Fig 1.23
Preston Patrick old meeting
house, built 1691.
[From a 19th-century
photograph by J J Hogg]

Fig 1.24
Colthouse meeting house,
built 1688.

Fig 1.25
Cartmel Height meeting
house, built 1677, now a
dwelling.

Fig 1.26
Swarthmoor meeting house,
built in 1688 onto an existing
dwelling.

As early as 1698 Friends had agreed to build a larger stable and to make a room over part of the stable as an occasional meeting room. This was finally finished in 1711 and the room put to use as a schoolroom for an already existing Quaker school (Fig 1.22). In the early period Quakers had perforce to be a self-sufficient community, providing financial support for their own poor, schooling and apprenticeships for the young, and care for the elderly. These community aspects are discussed further in Chapter 3.

At Brigflatts the stable, subsequently enlarged, is on the opposite side of the lane leading to the meeting house, and borders the Quaker burial ground, which has been in continuous use since 1660. Together with the meeting house and the 17th-century farmhouse further down the lane, the home of Richard Robinson, they constitute a striking survival from the early days of the Society of Friends.

There are four other early meeting houses from this area of Cumbria that form a group with Brigflatts, showing the influence of the local vernacular. All are of two storeys and contain a full-height meeting room with a gallery at one end. All except one have substantial stone porches, witnessing to the weather experienced on the west side of the Pennines.

The original meeting house at Preston Patrick of 1691, eight miles from Brigflatts, was demolished and rebuilt in the 19th century. A surviving photograph (Fig 1.23) shows a very similar outer appearance to Brigflatts, the windows being placed almost identically, but with only a flimsy porch. There is evidence to suggest that the internal arrangement was also similar, with the ministers' stand on the long wall, but the gallery was approached by an external staircase, seen on the right of the picture.

At Colthouse, a small hamlet on the opposite side of the valley from Hawkshead in Cumbria, is a meeting house of 1688 (Fig 1.24) with a gabled two-storey porch rather larger than that at Brigflatts. The upper room is approached by a stair internal to the porch and has a mullioned two-light casement above, with leaded glazing. Inside there is a gallery with the women's meeting room beneath, concealed by sliding sash shutters. The walls are roughcast and the roof of slate. The tall sash windows on the left, which light the meeting room, were added in 1790, although original mullioned and transomed windows remain on the left wall (above the ministers' stand) and at the rear.

The porch in the old meeting house at Cartmel Height, high above the Kent estuary in Cumbria, is much more similar in structure to that at Brigflatts (Fig 1.25). The arched doorway is echoed in the arch of the upper window and there are benches on both sides of the porch. The building dates from 1677 and the attached cottage from 1712: the windows are not original, having been altered in 1772. The meeting in this isolated spot had varying fortunes through 250 years and the building was finally sold in 1922, since when it has been a cottage called 'Barrow Wife'.

The fourth of these meeting houses is that built at Swarthmoor, Cumbria, on a site and with money given by George Fox in 1687. The gift was accompanied by the exhortation, 'I would have the meeting place large, for Truth may increase'.[8] The walls are roughcast and the porch only a single storey. The structure on the right of the porch derives from the original house on the site to which the substantial meeting room has been added. The entrance porch leads to a corridor which separates the women's meeting room, on the right, from the main meeting room on the left. This necessitates an arrangement not seen elsewhere, where two sets of shutters, one on either side of the corridor, are needed to enable the two rooms to be linked for large meetings for worship. A similar arrangement of shutters is seen a little further south in the 1692 meeting house at Yealand, Lancashire.

The photograph (Fig 1.26) shows only two of the three large windows which light the meeting room and which were installed in 1829 but now have 20th-century glazing. To the right of the porch are original three-light mullioned windows lighting the women's meeting room and the gallery.

The character of early meeting houses

All these early Quaker meeting houses date from the penal period (before 1689) or from the early period of toleration (1689–1705). As often as not they have been built by Friends themselves with only the pattern of local buildings to guide their construction. They are therefore modest structures which often reflect the vernacular buildings which are around them, not deliberately simple but simply innocent of architectural pretension. They belong either in small towns and villages or in the open countryside and so it is no surprise that they are similar to modest cottages or small houses of the period and they may even be adapted from such structures. This is probably not the result of a deliberate policy of 'hiding in plain sight', as Quakers set great store by meeting openly: there are plenty of examples of meeting houses being built within sight of the parish church, as at Alton. Where meeting houses are apparently hidden away, this is most likely to have been a result of the scarcity of building land on the street front in the crowded towns and villages of early modern England.

The vast majority of these meeting houses are rectangular in plan with most of the windows on one long wall, which also contains the single entrance to the meeting room set centrally, or, in examples with more than three bays, asymmetrically. Nowhere do we see the two entrances set at either end of the façade, which is typical of early meeting houses of other denominations. When seated in the meeting house, advice from 1678 was that 'women do sit on one side of the meeting-place, apart from the men' and this seems to have been standard practice, as in many parish churches.

Although these meeting houses may be in part on two storeys, the meeting room itself is always of full height. Whereas in the long-wall meeting houses of other denominations the pulpit usually resides on the long wall, the analogous structure in early Quaker meeting houses, the ministers' stand, is most often found on the short gable wall. The gallery, where there is one, is arranged opposite the stand.

It is remarkable the frequency with which we find chimneys and fireplaces in these buildings, at a time when churches and meeting houses were in general unheated. However, with the exception of north Cumbria, where they are found adjacent to the ministers' stand, fireplaces are usually found in the women's meeting room or in a part of the building that was at some point, maybe long after the original construction, occupied as a dwelling.

As we have seen, these early meeting houses have rarely survived unchanged. Enlargement of windows and the installation of sashes is the most common change. Meeting houses which originally consisted of a single full-height room may also have seen the installation of a gallery to increase seating and the division of the space vertically into two rooms separated by moveable shutters so that the men's and women's meetings for business could take place at the same time.

Many early meeting houses have not survived because the Quaker meetings for which they were built did not themselves survive the decline of the Society in subsequent centuries. Of the 35 early meeting houses detailed in David Butler's *Quaker Meeting Houses of the Lake Counties*,[9] only 11 still contain active Quaker meetings; the rest have been demolished or survive, like those at Askwith and Height, as residences. The other striking statistic is that 15 of those 35 were rebuilt either on the same or a different site, part of a national phenomenon known as the Great Rebuilding in which earlier materials, such as timber, earth and thatch were replaced with the more durable masonry, brick and slate.

Notes

1 Penney 1907, 37. Pardshaw Crag is just above the site of the current meeting house.
2 From the Epistle of Yearly Meeting, 1675.
3 I am grateful to Laurel Phillipson for this suggestion.
4 The other two were at Almeley Wootton and Faringdon.
5 Minutes of Tottenham Monthly Meeting, 1692 (as quoted in Butler 1999b, 215).
6 Penney 1907, 113.
7 Butler 1999a, 491, 493; Penney 1907, 113.
8 Ibid, 340.
9 Butler 1978.

2 The vain fashions of this world

Early meeting houses to 1715: Part 2

Town meeting houses

Most of the meeting houses described so far are from rural locations, where economic and other changes are less liable to have led to rebuilding or demolition. Towns and cities where Quakers were numerous from the early days, such as Bristol, Colchester, London, Norwich and York have had their meeting houses rebuilt several times so that no early examples remain.

It is worth mentioning at this point the first purpose-built meeting house in Bristol of 1670 because, unusually, we have a contemporary drawing of it in James Millerd's *An exact delineation of the famous citty of Bristol ...* of 1673. Millerd shows 'The Meeting houses' as a building of two storeys with a hipped roof culminating in a large central lantern (Fig 2.1). Such an elegant design survives in England only in the later meeting house at Bristol (*see* pages 50–1), although top-lit meeting houses were not unknown, particularly on cramped inner-city sites, as can be seen in Jacobsz's engraving of the main meeting house in Amsterdam, adapted for use around 1695 (Fig 2.2). Square-plan meeting houses with central lanterns were built early in Philadelphia and Newport, Rhode Island, which Hinshaw has suggested are due to the influence of the Bristol design.[1] Quakers have returned to the advantages of top light in meeting houses in the 21st century, perhaps because such a design provides an architectural metaphor for the light of the spirit.

A clear example of Quaker builders using as a model another dissenting meeting house was in Norwich, where in 1694 the Friends decided to build a second meeting house across the river and outside the city walls, where they had had a burial ground since 1670. This Gildencroft Meeting House was finished in 1698 and followed closely the plan used for the Old Meeting House built for the congregationalists in Colegate, nearby, in 1693 (Fig 2.3). Both were large square-form buildings in brick with hipped roofs and with a front decorated with five pilasters and pierced with two levels of windows. The Quaker building had less decoration, only a central doorway and many more windows (14 as against 8 at the Old Meeting); inside, the pulpit and the ministers' stand occupied the same position on the wall opposite the entrance, with a gallery on three sides, at the Old Meeting, but only to either side at Gildencroft. After the rebuilding of the Goat Lane meeting house in 1826 (*see* page 68) Gildencroft fell out of use for long periods and was almost entirely destroyed by bombing in 1942.

The oldest purpose-built meeting house in continuous occupation comes from the county town of Hertford. There had been a meeting at Hertford since 1655, but Quakers had met in Friends' houses, which had occasioned a number of prosecutions under the Conventicle Act, for which several Friends were imprisoned and had been threatened with

Fig 2.1
Bristol meeting house of 1670 as seen on Millerd's map of 1673.

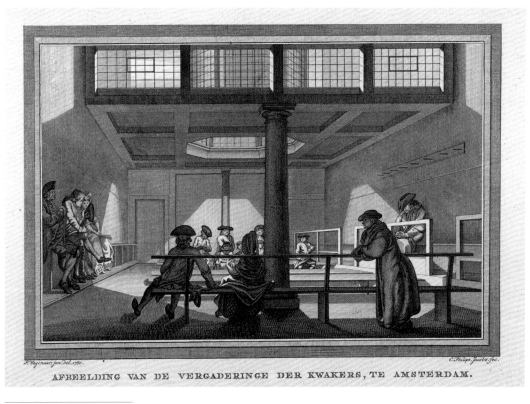

AFBEELDING VAN DE VERGADERINGE DER KWAKERS, TE AMSTERDAM.

Fig 2.2
The interior of the
Amsterdam meeting house
in Keizersgracht, acquired
in 1695, showing the top
lighting and central lantern.
[From an engraving of 1780
by Caspar Jacobsz]

transportation. Indeed, when the decision was taken to build a meeting house in 1669, at least 21 members of the meeting were still imprisoned. Nevertheless, a plot of land on Back Street was bought from a Friend and a building erected to a thoroughly domestic design which would have fitted with the other houses in the street, but which contrasts with the elegance of the Bristol and Norwich designs.

The meeting house has a rectangular plan and is built of red brick with a complex tiled roof. Facing the street, the frontage is topped by two gables from which roof ridges run backwards to meet the single ridge which runs across the rear of the building. Both front gables contain a small casement window, while at the lower level there were originally three windows flanked by two doors; the left-hand door and all the windows have been partially bricked up, with small two-light windows with leaded panes remaining at the top. A similar window lies over the right-hand doorway, which is the entrance to the building. All the openings are topped by shallow brick arches (Fig 2.4).

The rear elevation contains two central unblocked windows which must look similar to the originals at the front, and again two doorways with two-paned windows above at either end, one of which, the right-hand one, has been bricked up. The roof slope to the rear also contains a small dormer at the left-hand end. From the rear the large chimney stack on the rear gable end dominates the view.

Entering through the main doorway, there is a lobby area running the whole width of the building, at the far end of which is a large hearth and

Fig 2.3
(a) (left) Gildencroft meeting house, Norwich of 1698 and (b) (right) The Old Meeting, Colegate of 1693. Was the second a model for the first? [Photographs taken by the late George Plunkett in 1934 and 1981 respectively]

Fig 2.4
Hertford meeting house (1669) from the north.

Fig 2.5
Hertford meeting house interior, facing the stand, rebuilt in 1717. The white metal posts and beams supporting the roof are an addition of the 1970s.

beyond it a stair leading to the gallery above. On the left a wooden partition with moveable shutters containing double doors separates the lobby from the main meeting room. In the gallery above – now divided into two rooms – is another large hearth and a similar partition and shutters. It is thought that the shutters are not original, but that the partition both upstairs and down may originally have been plastered.

What is clear is that during its first half-century the building was changed a number of times: it may have been damaged by the authorities in 1684; the external doors at the north end were changed to windows in 1717 and at the same time sashes were fitted in the other windows which are no longer there. The current ministers' stand cannot have been built in its present form until the removal of the north doors. This stand is a very impressive structure, particularly for its period, with fixed benches with boarded backs at four levels and doors at the highest level. The meeting room itself is spacious because of its height: a substantial freestanding timber post in the centre of the room supports the timbers of the roofs, a characteristic it shares with its near contemporary at Ifield. Although the floor is boarded it retains the stone slab which supported the heating stove which warmed this meeting house, as countless others, in the 19th century (Fig 2.5).

In 1738 a separate single-storey women's meeting house was built in a similar style in the front yard. This remains, halved in size by road widening in the 1930s, and rebuilt to serve as a classroom.

Other large towns that retain meeting houses built during the first 50 years of the Quaker movement include Worcester, where Quakers undertook their first purpose-built meeting house in 1701 on a site just

Fig 2.6
*Worcester meeting house,
built 1701.*

outside the medieval city walls. It is a single-storey building built of orange brick, with a painted brick plinth with an elegantly symmetrical south-facing entrance front (Fig 2.6). In the centre is a pedimented porch with double doors and to either side are two 20-paned sash windows under shallow brick arches. The hipped roof is of slate and on the north side there are two symmetrically placed smaller windows with the other two openings blind. The entrance originally gave directly onto the single meeting room with the ministers' stand on the north wall. However, when a women's meeting room with two classrooms beneath was built at the east end in the 1820s, the meeting room was reoriented with the stand on the west wall and a gallery on the east, the structure of which survives. The interior was divided up and repurposed in the 1980s and the internal furnishings have gone.

These same alterations included a housing association development to the east of the meeting house, complementing on the west side the three 18th-century terraced cottages erected to house needy Friends. The whole, with its cobbled forecourt shielded from the street by a substantial wall, creates a peaceful campus-like oasis in the heart of the city.

The other town meeting house that deserves mention at this point is that at Lancaster. Its architectural history is more complex than the previous three, but the meeting house which survives retains much of the design of that built in 1708. Quakers first built on this large site south of the castle in 1677, which seems remarkable given that during the 1670s and 1680s hundreds of Quakers were imprisoned in the castle for various offences under the Clarendon Code. Even though Meeting House Lane (then Kiln Lane) was not a major route within the town, the meeting house was certainly not secreted away!

The rebuilding of 1708 was occasioned by the need for more space in a building which housed the gatherings of the Yearly Meeting for the Northern Counties from 1699. The plan was to provide two meeting houses, divided unusually by a solid wall, not the customary shutters, within a rectangular single-storey building, probably with a small porch. Originally of six bays with the doorway in the third bay, it was extended in both directions to its present nine bays by further building in 1779 and 1789. It is constructed of sandstone rubble faced with roughcast render with a roof of grey sandstone at the front and slates at the rear (Fig 2.7). The south-facing front now has eight tall 12-paned sash windows, three on the left lighting the women's meeting room and the five on the right the main meeting room. The gable at the east end contains a handsome Venetian window of 1779, and the two-storey porch achieved its current form in 1789, with doors to both meeting rooms, the left-hand one reusing an old lintel with the date 1677.

Fig 2.7
Lancaster meeting house from the south, showing the porch of 1789 and the central bays.

Fig 2.8
Lancaster, interior of men's meeting room in 1900. [From a photograph in Lancaster meeting house]

Leading from the porch was a lobby with gallery above, which could be reached by stairs at the end of the lobby. This west gallery would have connected with the upper room in the porch, as at Brigflatts, and would have been contiguous with the north gallery in the main meeting room. Between the lobby and the main meeting room is a screen which may once have had moveable shutters.

There exists a photo of the main meeting room in 1900 (Fig 2.8) which shows the ministers' stand with the Venetian window over it, a gallery on the north wall lit above by a mullioned window, and also the heating stove with its vertical chimney. This gallery was subsequently removed; only the dado panelling on the north and east walls remains of the original furnishings. The women's meeting room was adapted in the 20th century to contain a kitchen and offices over, although part retains its full height.

Jordans

Lancaster plays an important part in early Quaker history as the site of the assizes and prison for the historic County Palatine, which at that time included the northern Cumbrian shore of Morecambe Bay and thus was closely linked to the areas of Westmorland where the events of 1652 played out – what is now called '1652 country'.[2] Another part of the country which has important links with early Quaker history is the area of Buckinghamshire and Oxfordshire surrounding the Chilterns. This is largely linked to the name of William Penn (1644–1718), who joined the Quakers in 1666 and, because of his connections at court and his founding of Pennsylvania, became an influential Quaker leader.

He is buried, together with his wives, Mary Springett, née Penington (1623–82), and Hannah Callowhill (1671–1726), in the Quaker burial ground at Jordans. In the 20th century this made Jordans a place of Quaker pilgrimage. Burials here have taken place since 1671, but the meeting house was not built until 1688, the meeting having previously been held at Hunger Hill, north of Beaconsfield, the home of Thomas Ellwood (1639–1714), friend of John Milton and editor of George Fox's *Journal*.

Jordans meeting house is a brick-built structure on a rectangular plan under a hipped tile roof. The west (entrance) front has a central

Fig 2.9
Jordans meeting house, built 1688, from the west, the 19th-century gravestones of William Penn and others on the left.

Fig 2.10
Jordans interior – the gallery.

Fig 2.11
Jordans interior – the main
meeting room with the stand,
showing the mid-18th-
century panelling obscuring
the earlier windows.

doorway with double doors surmounted by an oblong two-light timber-mullioned fanlight. To the north are two wooden casement windows with brick arches lighting the main meeting room, whereas to the south the building is divided into two storeys and there are two smaller windows: all the windows contain leaded lights and, with the exception of the fanlight, have external shutters. In essence this is the usual plan for an early long-wall meeting house, as we have seen at Swarthmoor and Brigflatts, but with a central rather than an off-centre doorway (Fig 2.9).

The door gives directly into the main meeting room, which has the ministers' stand at one end and, at the other, a gallery with a partition of sliding shutters, which has acted as the women's meeting room (Fig 2.10), above a lobby area with a side entrance and large open fireplace, again with a partition of sliding shutters. During the closure of the meeting, from 1798 to 1910, this end of the meeting house was used as a caretaker's cottage.

This main meeting room has a wooden panelled dado which rises over the ministers' stand, which is raised on two steps, partially obscuring the window above. This may indicate that the current furnishings are a later addition, dating perhaps from the first half of the 18th century. The floor is of orange-red bricks laid on bare earth. The bench on the stand stretches across the whole wall, although the rail in front and the bench in front of that only extend across half the width. On the two flanking walls there are also fixed benches (Fig 2.11).

There was originally stabling to the rear of the building, but this area has been rebuilt several times; the most recent rebuilding, which provided excellent modern meeting facilities, followed a fire in 2005.

The rows of gravestones outside the meeting house which commemorate the early Friends buried here were not erected until the mid-19th century, and since there was no record of the position of the early burials, the placing of the stones is dependent only on oral tradition. To one side is the modern burial ground, which was set out in 1937 by the architect Hubert Lidbetter and which uniquely has the gravestones arranged in concentric circles rather than in rows.

Reuse of old buildings

Jordans was built on the eve of the arrival of toleration: in 1689 meeting houses could be legally registered for the first time since 1672. The late 1680s and 1690s therefore was a time when meeting house building was perhaps at its height. But these newly registered meeting houses were not all new built. That at Great Yarmouth contains perhaps the oldest foundations of any meeting house. Quakers in the town bought in 1694 a plot of land on which stood the remains of a 14th-century building which had contained a separated part of an Augustinian Friary based at Gorleston, on the other side of the river Yare. This was adapted to serve as a meeting house in that year, but the structure that now stands on the site is the result of rebuilding in 1807. The medieval origins are clearest in the basement area, excavated in 1981, where the medieval flint and stone walls are revealed, together with four old door or window openings filled with brick (Fig 2.12). The other remarkable feature is the gallery, now walled off from the meeting house, but a perfectly preserved example of an early 19th-century structure, with a raked floor and fixed benches (Fig 2.13).

At Brant Broughton (pronounced 'Bruton') in Lincolnshire, Quakers who had been worshipping in the house of Londoner Thomas Robinson were given by him a timber-framed thatched barn with a cottage attached at the south end for use as a meeting house. The barn was largely rebuilt in local Ancaster stone in about 1701: the original meeting house door is surmounted with a plaque inscribed with R over T+S (for Thomas and Sarah Robinson) 1701. A second door in this frontage, formerly that of the cottage, now leads into the meeting house lobby. At the more northerly end are two wooden mullioned and transomed window casements with square leaded lights and beneath them a brick mounting block. A small stable block in red brick was added to this north end of the building in 1776 (now converted to a children's room). The south gable end and much of the rear wall were rebuilt around 1800 in brick, and this may have been the point at which the original thatch was replaced with pantiles (Fig 2.14).

Further land was added to the site for a burial ground in 1727, and sometime in the late 19th or early 20th century an open carriage shed with cast iron supports and a curved corrugated iron roof was placed at the south end of the main driveway.

Fig 2.12
Great Yarmouth meeting house interior – basement showing medieval wall with bricked up openings on the left.

Fig 2.13
Great Yarmouth interior – gallery showing 19th-century fixed benches on a stepped floor.

Fig 2.14
Brant Broughton meeting house, built 1701, showing the entrance front with brick mounting block in the foreground together with the entrance to the later stable block on the right. The far door is that of the original cottage.

Fig 2.15
Brant Broughton interior viewed from the gallery.

Much change has taken place in the meeting house over the years; however, with the exception of the incorporation of the former cottage into the meeting house, there seems to have been relatively little change to the interior. The cottage retains both a bread oven and a fireplace downstairs, where there is a fixed bench against one wall; a small winding stair leads upwards to the gallery where there is another fireplace and there are benches set out. The wooden partition between the cottage and the meeting room contains shutters at both levels, the lower ones hinge into the lobby whereas the upper ones now, unusually, hinge into the meeting room.

The meeting room itself has a wooden dado to sill level with fixed benches round parts of the walls, together with an extra short bench in front of the original meeting house door with a high back to shield from draughts. The stand at the far end has a bench which occupies the whole wall and is raised one step with a plain panelled front, pierced at either side with two openings; between these openings a fixed bench is set at floor level. All the woodwork in the meeting house is painted white, which is not likely to be original (Fig 2.15). It is thought that Quakers used paint only on the outside of their meeting houses, the wood within was polished or varnished.

Fig 2.16
Airton meeting house from the burial ground, with the meeting house itself on the right and the barn on the left.

At Airton in Malhamdale, the meeting house also may have had a previous existence, perhaps as an agricultural building of an earlier date. It was rebuilt in the 1690s by Quaker weavers William and Alice Ellis, and has an entrance doorway with arched lintel inscribed with their initials (WAE 1700). This entrance is quite unusually on the side of the building away from the road and facing the burial ground. Above the doorway is a flat stone canopy on stone brackets. Left of the door are two two-light mullioned windows lighting the meeting room, and to the right a single two-light window to the room beneath the gallery, with one smaller two-light mullioned window above. The structure, which is of coursed rubble with quoins, is contiguous with the neighbouring cottage, which houses a resident friend, and with a converted barn, perhaps originally a stable, which provides hostel accommodation (Fig 2.16).

Internally the meeting room is oriented with the ministers' stand, possibly of a later date, on the left, and to the right the original oak screen with moveable shutters and a doorway which divided off the women's meeting room. Above this, and reached by narrow stairs on the other side of the room, is the gallery with an oak-panelled front. Both the gallery and the lower meeting room have stone fireplaces.

Friends at Bridport in Dorset were meeting in the 1690s in a barn, part of the current site, which is a complex of late medieval tenements around a courtyard, given to the meeting in 1697 and containing both a meeting house and almshouses. On the street, only the large windows distinguish the meeting house from the adjacent houses, although there was at one time a street door direct into the meeting room. Above the pitched roof at the front can be seen the ridge of the main meeting house roof (Fig 2.17). The internal furnishings were largely removed in the 1950s, leaving a high-ceilinged room with the remains of one of the galleries at the far end.

Interestingly, the almshouses, which are owned by a separate trust, continue in use on one side of the courtyard, which contains the meeting house entrance and which is approached by a passageway through

Fig 2.17
Bridport meeting house from the street. On the left, with the signboard over, is Porch House, with the way through to the courtyard: the meeting house is the building beyond with the two large casement windows with a noticeboard between.

neighbouring Porch House. Beyond this, and surrounded by tall stone walls, is the former garden which has since 1811 been the Quaker burial ground.

Meeting houses in smaller towns

Quakers at Stourbridge in the West Midlands built their first meeting house in 1689 on land given by Abraham Crowley, a local Quaker ironmonger. It is a brick-built single-storey building with a tiled roof on a rectangular plan, originally with the doorway on the long wall between the existing two three-light casement windows with leaded panes that light the meeting room. At an early point the structure was lengthened and the door moved to the gable end. This extension contains a similar two-light window and above it a dormer window in the eaves. Beyond this the original structure becomes obscured by 20th-century additions (Fig 2.18).

From inside, the gable end wall can be seen with a window originally above the entrance door. The meeting room is reached through a lobby, now the library, with above it the gallery which juts into the meeting room and is supported on two pillars. The meeting room has the central ministers' stand at the far end, raised two steps, with fitted benches at ground level either side, returning along both side walls. Viewed from the meeting room, the gallery has a flat balustraded front with hinged shutters behind to close off the upper room, which has a fireplace and is lit by the dormer window.

At Nailsworth in Gloucestershire the meeting house was registered in 1689 but was possibly built a little earlier. It is attached and at right angles to the adjacent house, but it is not clear whether it was new-built or adapted from an earlier building on the site: a change in roof line highlights the possible transition from old to new. The front elevation faces a courtyard and has an arched central doorway with a central keystone and spandrels framed by a square edge. To the left of the

Fig 2.18
Stourbridge meeting house, built 1688, with (above) a photograph taken during renovations, the brickwork showing the original position of the door on the long wall.

Fig 2.19 (above left) Nailsworth meeting house, the courtyard front. The changes in stonework and roofline indicate where the original cottage gives way to the building of 1689.

Fig 2.20 (above right) Painswick meeting house, built 1706, showing the gable end with the door added in 1793/4.

door is a pair of small mullioned windows with diamond-leaded casements and above this, to the left, a similar mullioned window which lights an upper room. To the right of the door, a larger opening has two pairs of mullioned and transomed windows with 20th-century metal casements with diamond panes (Fig 2.19). This elevation shares some features with the earlier meeting house in Cirencester, which are obscured there by later rebuilding. The side elevation reveals twin roofs ending in gables, each with a lower window, one of which is blocked.

The meeting room is now entered via a draught lobby and is arranged with the stand at the far end. This, the dado panelling and the partition with shutters which separates the room from the library essentially belong to the early 19th century. The upper room above the library has never been used as a gallery but does have its original floor and a window (now blocked) which once gave secondary light into the meeting room.

Nearby in Gloucestershire is another early meeting house, built at Painswick in 1705/6 on the edge of this Cotswold wool town. The rectangular-plan building is of local limestone, with a tall steeply pitched roof which houses a number of attic rooms. The south elevation, overlooking the valley, is of three bays with the original entrance, now blocked, in the centre framed by two large 24-paned sash windows. The current entrance in the gable end was formed during modifications in 1794 and is topped with a stone hood on wooden brackets. Above it are two casement windows lighting rooms on the attic floor. These are matched in the other gable by two 12-paned sash windows (Fig 2.20).

The door leads into the narrowest of lobbies which stretches the whole width of the building but is scarcely four feet wide. It is separated from the meeting room by a panelled partition which intriguingly contains shutters; on the right a stairway leads to the upper attic floor which contained the women's meeting room. The main meeting room has a short ministers' stand at the far end with a panelled front, a plain deal dado behind, and fixed benches at either side. The dado running round the other walls is painted and rises above the stand at the far end.

At the other side of the Cotswolds in Oxfordshire, Burford meeting house, built in 1708, also has the women's meeting room in an attic. The

Fig 2.21
Burford meeting house, built
1708, with the extension of
1981 to the right.

Fig 2.22
Burford, the interior from the
stand, showing the gallery
and fixed benches with the
door to the new extension.

building is on a square plan and is built on a former orchard at the rear of the Bull Inn on the High Street. It is constructed in coursed stone rubble with ashlar surrounds to the door and windows. The main entrance gives onto a small burial ground and is approached by three steps; either side are two very tall 24-paned sash windows. The roof is of Cotswold stone slates and is half-hipped (Fig 2.21).

The unique feature is the gallery, which occupies two sides of the room and is supported on wooden posts with a simple rail and posts at the front. It is reached by a stair on the right of the entrance and has another boxed-in stair leading from it to the attic room, an addition of the 1730s, in the corner. At the lower level the walls have fixed benches with a dado behind, which rises over the former stand on the left-hand wall. Some of the benches have been removed from the right-hand wall to effect an entrance to the modern extension beyond (Fig 2.22). The whole bears some similarities, in its height and its prominent gallery, to Adderbury, 24 miles away.

Two Cornish meeting houses

Although Cornwall was evangelised by a number of Friends, including George Fox, who was imprisoned in Launceston Castle for six months in 1656, Quakerism never took as strong a hold in the county as did Methodism a century later. The oldest meeting house in Cornwall is at Marazion and was built in 1688 and opened in January 1689: it has the appearance of a vernacular cottage (Fig 2.23). It is of granite rubble roughly coursed together with some cob at the rear and is on a rectangular plan. The entrance was originally in the middle of the long side, but this was changed, the entrance door removed to the gable end, and three sash windows placed on the south side, probably in 1742. Inside is a single room, open to the rafters with a dado round the walls and the original ministers' stand at the east end. This consists of a central bench with moulded ends on a dais, raised up three or four steps, with wall benches at a lower level either side and a rail in front with flattened column balusters and square newel posts with knob finials. This design is similar to that at Farfield. Unfortunately, the door to the modern extension now stands next to the bench on the north side, somewhat breaking the symmetry.

Fig 2.23
Marazion meeting house, built 1688, showing the gable-end entrance created in the 18th century.

By far the most famous of Cornish meeting houses, that at Come-to-Good in Kea parish, was built a little later than Marazion. The hamlet has a remote location on the hills above the River Fal a little to the south of Truro, on the road leading to the King Harry ferry. The meeting was founded in the early 1650s and had been surviving in rented buildings until 1710. The meeting house built that year is thoroughly in the Cornish vernacular, being built of whitewashed cob on stone rubble footings and with a steep thatched roof which extends to one side to include the later linhay or stable. Like Marazion, the building faces south and originally had its entrance in the middle of that side; the sides of the porch remain. The windows either side of the former doorway are original three-light windows in oak frames and lintels and with external shutters; they are of a slightly archaic design and may have been reused from another building. There were also originally windows high up in both end walls but only that at the west end survives (Fig 2.24).

The meeting room is now entered via a modern extension, where a plank door gives entrance to the single barn-like room, open to the roof, with the ministers' stand straight ahead. This is curiously not exactly in the middle of the far wall and is of the short type seen at Ettington, a bench raised by two steps with a boarded back, all in pine. In front of this is a pine panel with square newels and a small fixed reading desk, with a plain bench in front. On either side the stand is flanked by fixed benches with a dado back which returns on both sides without covering the whole wall (Fig 2.25).

Originally there was no gallery against the west wall but this was added after less than 10 years and is supported by two wooden pillars which are thought to be refashioned from a ship's mast. The gallery is fronted with pine in which is a blocked door (the culmination of the original stair) and three openings with a simple balustrade. There are no shutters to isolate the gallery for the women's business meeting. The gallery is now reached by a stair in the north-west corner (Fig 2.26).

Despite its relatively late date, this meeting house, with its isolated situation and picturesque exterior, is to our age remarkably evocative of

Fig 2.24 (above)
Come-to-Good meeting house.
Note the side walls and roof of
the former porch still in place
and the prominent linhay, or
stable.

Fig 2.25 (above right)
Come-to-Good, the interior
taken from under the gallery
and showing the stand.

Fig 2.26 (right)
Come-to-Good, the interior
from the stand, showing the
gallery open and without
shutters with the original
door on the right.

the situation in which the earliest Quakers worshipped, in agricultural
buildings and simple vernacular meeting houses built often with their
own labour, and as such has become something of a tourist attraction.

The American meeting house

Quakers had been building meeting houses in the Americas since the
late 1650s to support the small groups of Friends in colonies stretching
from Rhode Island to Virginia and the Carolinas. Before the creation of
Pennsylvania in 1681, another colony was founded under Quaker auspices
in 1677 in West Jersey. The first town was at Burlington on the east bank
of the Delaware river. The meeting house built there in 1683 had the
novel form of a brick-built hexagon with a six-sided roof, leading, as at
Bristol, to a large central lantern (Fig 2.27). The seating was apparently
in four blocks separated by two aisles. It was not until 1696 that it was
enlarged at the rear and a ministers' stand was built on the long wall of
this extension.

FRIENDS' MEETING HOUSE, BURLINGTON, N. J.

Fig 2.27
Burlington, New Jersey,
old meeting house of 1683,
showing the hexagonal form.

The earliest meeting house still surviving is that at Third Haven on the eastern shore of Chesapeake Bay in Maryland, built about 1682, although today existing in the enlarged form caused by rebuilding at the end of the 18th century. It is a typical long-wall meeting house built in wood with external weatherboarding; the original entrance was on the long side, although it is now in the gable end (Fig 2.28).

Another early long-wall meeting house survives at Flushing in the New York borough of Queens. This is again of wooden construction, covered with wooden shingles with a hipped roof and was built initially in 1694 for a group of Quakers who had emigrated from Holland. This building too was extended in the 18th century.

A meeting house in the area to the west of Philadelphia which was settled by Welsh Quakers shows how this long-wall design developed. Radnor meeting house was built in 1718 in stone as a single-storey three-bay meeting house with a steeply pitched roof. It contained a single meeting room, but the needs of the women's business meeting led in 1722 to the addition of a smaller room at the side (Fig 2.29).

Fig 2.28 (below left)
Third Haven meeting house.

Fig 2.29 (below right)
Radnor meeting house,
showing the women's
meeting house attached at
the right.

Fig 2.30
Exeter meeting house,
showing an early version of
the side-by-side design.

Eventually this led in the 1750s to the construction of meeting houses like that at Exeter, Pennsylvania (1758), where the men's and women's meeting houses are of identical size and side by side under a single roof (Fig 2.30). Each meeting house has its own entrance; the ministers' stand is on the far wall and they are separated by a full-height wooden screen of sliding panels. This was to become the standard American meeting house design for the next century.

The early Quaker meeting house

As we shall see, British Quakers did occasionally use this American design, as at Kendal and Darlington (*see* Chapter 4), but more usually the women's meeting room was smaller than that for the men. It was either completely separate (as at Hertford and Adderbury), upstairs (as at Burford and Painswick) or separated from the main meeting room by a partition with shutters. In these early meeting houses it could either be the lower room of a two-storey structure (as at Swarthmoor, Colthouse and Airton) or be in the gallery or upper room (as at Alton and Stourbridge).

Having surveyed a larger number of meeting houses in a larger variety of situations, we can see that early meeting houses are not always of the simplest possible design and that although the vernacular style appears to dominate, particularly in the countryside, designs with some elements of architectural fashion can be found, particularly in towns. Here, symmetrical frontages and central doorways are more frequent, particularly towards the end of our period, as at Gildencroft and Worcester. However, the position of the entrance door on the long wall is almost invariable; when it is found elsewhere, as in the two Cornish examples, it is almost always the result of later changes.

Although there was no coordinated planning of meeting houses, it is clear that Friends were aware of what other Friends were building, presumably through visiting other meeting houses. The installation of ministers' stands where one was not built originally is evidence of this.

There is also some evidence that Quakers were aware of what other dissenters were building, as at Gildencroft.

Later replacement of casement windows with the newer and more fashionable sashes is a frequent post-construction change in many meeting houses. Sash windows certainly had the functional advantage of letting more light into the large full-height rooms that Quakers were soon building. Their introduction will likely have occurred through emulation of other buildings, either secular or religious. Although sash windows were first used in England in the 1670s, there are no Quaker meeting houses built with them before about 1700. Replacement generally took place during the 18th century, although in some places it was delayed even longer.

Notes

1 Hinshaw 2001, 24.
2 The meeting of George Fox with the Westmorland Seekers in 1652 (see the Introduction) came, in the late 19th century, to be seen as the founding moment of Quakerism. The area, historically in the West Riding and Lancashire, over which George Fox travelled at this time, stretching from Pendle Hill in the south to Kendal in the north and east to west from Sedbergh to Ulverston, came to be known as '1652 country' and was the destination of numerous Quaker pilgrimages in the 20th century.

3 A subdued but self-contained community

Quaker buildings 1715–1815

At the beginning of the 18th century, Quakerism had already passed its peak in England and Wales. There were still perhaps 40,000 Quakers in some 600 congregations around the country, perhaps 0.75 per cent of the population, concentrated in Yorkshire and the North West, the Midlands, some parts of East Anglia and around the capital, with Bristol an outlier in the South West. They were now the smallest of the major groups of dissenters who had been founded or flourished in the previous century.

Most, if not all, of the first generation, those who had been transformed by the missionary work of the 1650s and 1660s, had died, and meetings largely consisted of their surviving families, people who had been brought up in a Quaker community, were content with their inheritance, but who had not necessarily undergone the same spiritual awakening as their parents and grandparents. There was no longer the hope that the whole of society might be transformed by the Quaker message. Friends felt themselves to be 'a remnant of Israel'[1] and turned inwards to protect themselves.

Friends might have felt isolated within their own country, but they retained lively links with Quakers in other parts of the world, particularly in the Americas and Ireland, both by exchange of correspondence and by intervisitation.

The Quaker distinctives – treating all equally, truth and integrity in business, simplicity of dress and lifestyle – were no longer the outward expressions of an inward transformation: they became the rule by which to live. Discipline was transformed from discipleship into a straitjacket.

The Society of Friends became more tightly organised and centralised. The Yearly Meeting, which met annually in London, operated a system of oversight which consisted in 'queries' to be answered by meetings and epistles sent back, exhorting Quakers to be faithful. Topics for epistles at this time focused on appealing to Friends to be careful in their education of the young, not to be seduced by the constantly changing fashions of society, and to return to obedience to the founding experience of the Light Within. Quakers were expected to wear 'plain dress', never quite the uniform illustrated by the Quaker Oats logo, but clothes in sombre colours and without unnecessary ornament. Formal membership was introduced in the 1730s, largely to make clear who was expected to support the Society financially and to whom individual meetings were obliged to offer support when need arose.

Roles within the Society also became more formalised. Meetings appointed elders to organise worship and overseers to provide pastoral care. Those with a special gift for ministry during worship were recorded centrally as ministers and were then freed to travel around the country and even abroad to offer their ministry to other Friends. They were also expected, if they were able, to preach in public to what Friends would have called 'the world's people'. Quakers retained the distinction, in contrast to other denominations, that all these roles remained open to both sexes. Quaker women ministers remained a curiosity for the public and could draw large crowds: it was one such that caused Dr Johnson to remark, 'a woman's preaching is like a dog's walking on his hind legs. It is not done well; but you are surprised to find it done at all.'[2]

As meetings became more dependent on recorded ministers, other ministry was inhibited and many meetings became customarily silent. In meeting houses the elders and overseers occupied the lower seats in the ministers' stand, the former effectively policing the worship.

Friends had always publicly dissociated themselves from those who did not behave in an appropriate manner by excessive drinking, immodesty or bad practice in business. This now became formalised in a process of disownment for these reasons and for violating other rules, particularly for supporting the established church, by paying tithes to the clergy or by marrying in church. This latter effectively enforced intermarriage only with other Quakers, and inevitably led to a drift away from the Society of the disaffected young. Throughout the century Quaker birth rates lagged behind death rates: this and the decreased emphasis on conversion of non-Quakers led to a slow decline in numbers across the century.

The Quaker reputation for truth and integrity became an advantage for those in business, initially largely in agriculture and the textile industry, as artisans or traders. Along with other dissenters they were prevented from entering the professions which depended on education to degree level and/or the swearing of an oath. Some entered the medical professions where education could be obtained in Scotland and the Netherlands or via apprenticeship. Quakers were involved early in the industrialisation of the metal trades, both as investors and owners, notably the Darbys of Coalbrookdale and the Lloyds of Dolobran, but also with iron and coal in South Wales and with lead in the North East.

Quakers became sources of capital as traders turned to banking as a sideline: it has been calculated that nearly 20 per cent of the first 100 English banks were Quaker owned,[3] including the precursors of both Barclays and Lloyds, and the Norwich-based Gurney's Bank. The existence of a network of meetings across the country to which ministers, in particular, would travel, and the extensive cousinage caused by intermarriage, both favoured the contacts which could lead to entrepreneurial opportunities and investment. Hence the birth of Quaker firms which became national brands – Allen & Hanbury, pharmaceutical manufacturers (1710s); Fry's of Bristol, chocolate manufacturers (1760s); and Ransome's of Ipswich, agricultural engineers (1789).

Simple structures continue

The building of meeting houses continued, with much of it being rebuilding of older and perhaps simpler premises. Nevertheless, new meeting houses could still be modest structures, such as that at

Fig 3.1
The exterior of Wallingford
meeting house.

Fig 3.2
The interior of Wallingford
meeting house.

Wallingford of 1724, built in brick at the rear of a cottage close to the centre of this small town on the Thames. The single meeting room is only 18ft (5.5m) by 24ft (7m), lit by 12-paned sash windows on three sides and with a small ministers' stand in the centre of the fourth side, similar to that at Ettington. There is a simple boarded wooden dado and built-in benches either side of the stand which extend round the two neighbouring walls. From the outside the most striking feature is the tall hipped roof with its clay tiles; a neat doorcase with a double door faces the entrance from the street, which is via a corridor running through the caretaker's cottage (Figs 3.1 and 3.2).

Of similar appearance is the somewhat larger meeting house, on an unusual square plan, built in 1733 at Earls Colne, near Colchester. This was the second meeting house on this site. It is brick-built with a pyramidal tiled roof and was originally lit by two small windows high in the wall at the front and at the back. Alterations over the last

Fig 3.3
Earls Colne meeting house
from the road.

Fig 3.4
The exterior of
Crawshawbooth meeting
house with the cottage
(subsuming the original
meeting house on the left).

Fig 3.5
The interior of
Crawshawbooth meeting
house from the gallery.

two centuries have several times changed the entrance to the building
(Fig 3.3). The single meeting room inside is 30ft (9m) square and retains
the long ministers' stand across one wall, reached at either side by four
steps with a bench beneath. There are two square columns in the centre
but no evidence of a division into two rooms. There was once a gallery
on the wall opposite the stand and, uniquely, an octagonal gallery above,
which still exists, concealed behind the present ceiling.

Evidence of 18th-century rebuilding can be seen in the meeting
house at Crawshawbooth near Rossendale in Lancashire. The original
meeting house of 1715 was likely a single-storey building above a stable
and is probably subsumed into the current cottage on the site. In 1723
a new meeting house was built beside the old stable. This is of squared
local sandstone with moulded stone window surrounds and a stone slate
roof; a porch roughly central to the structure shelters the entrance. The

main meeting room is lit at the front by two mullioned and transomed windows of six panes each with diamond-shaped leaded lights, and by a single similar window to the rear. To the left of the porch are two smaller mullioned windows which light the gallery and a lower small meeting room, rather similar to the arrangement at Brigflatts. There is also an external stone stair leading to the cottage (Fig 3.4).

Inside, a passage, separated from the meeting room by a low panelled wall, runs straight forward to the stone steps which lead to a balustraded gallery on the left. On the right is the main meeting room with a ministers' stand across the whole wall, but with two large fixed benches with panelled backs at the upper level and below them two fixed benches with balustraded backs. Access to the stand is in the centre and at either side. At one end of the stand there is a book cupboard with panelled door set into a blocked window opening (Fig 3.5). All meetings were encouraged to keep a library of Quaker books, and appropriate volumes were distributed from London: book cupboards are found in a number of 18th-century meeting houses.

There are fixed benches around the other three sides of the meeting space. Underneath the gallery is a smaller women's meeting room separated from the main room by double shutters which can be raised on either side to connect the rooms. This room has simple fixed seating with panelled backs and a blocked fireplace with a plain stone mantel.

Another humble structure from quite late in the century is that at Coanwood, near Haltwhistle in Northumbria, now in the ownership of the Historic Chapels Trust. This was built in 1760 by Cuthbert Wigham, a local landowner who had been converted to Quakerism some 25 years before. The building is of squared stone with rusticated quoins and dressings and is of a typical plan, rectangular of four bays with the entrance set in the third bay and fixed 12-paned windows. The roof is of stone at the eaves but of slate for the most part (Fig 3.6).

Inside, the floor is flagged and the original simple wooden benches remain. These provide for a modicum of comfort since their backs are raked. Some of the central benches are shortened, presumably to allow room for a central stove, and the rearmost bench by the door has a panelled back to minimise draughts. At this time men would still have sat on one side of the room and women on the other. The ministers' stand is

Fig 3.6
The exterior of Coanwood meeting house.

Fig 3.7
The interior of Coanwood meeting house.

raised by three steps and backed by a panelled dado with a simple rail in front with a central entrance. At the other end of the meeting room is a panelled partition with the usual top-hinged shutters dividing off the women's meeting room, to which access is gained by a central door (Fig 3.7).

Quaker elegance

These four are relatively unpretentious vernacular buildings, but at this and later periods Quaker meeting houses were not always so. The meeting house at Stafford is a neat example of an architecturally polite building. Built in 1730 to replace a 17th-century building on another site, it has a frontage with the entrance placed off-centre in its four-bay brick façade. The three casement windows (now unhappily modern replacements) are large but set high to avoid distraction and are topped with flat arches in rubbed brick with keystones. The door has a pedimented canopy topped with a vertical oval bulls-eye window, with a distinctive date stone above (Fig 3.8).

The interior has a gallery to one side facing the stand. The walls are panelled to head height, rising above the central ministers' stand which has a panelled front behind the lower fixed seats. The stand does not take up the whole wall and is approached from both sides by three steps. Stairs at the rear, concealed behind a door, rise to the stepped gallery from which the attic room above, said to have been the women's meeting room (as at Burford), can be reached by further stairs.

The elegant meeting house at Long Sutton, Somerset, of 1717 is also a rebuilding, brought about by a generous legacy from a local Quaker landowner resident in London, William Steele. On a site across the road from the former meeting house, a rectangular-plan structure of three bays was built of coursed blue lias stone with a Welsh slate roof. On both the long sides there is a wide doorway with double doors set in a moulded timber frame with a deep semi-circular hood together with two sash windows, each of 18 small panes with external timber shutters (Fig 3.9). One entrance is from the road and the other from the burial ground to the rear.

These doors both lead into a flagged entrance passage with a stair leading to the gallery above. The main room, almost square, has a

Fig 3.8 (below left)
The exterior of Stafford
meeting house.

Fig 3.9 (below right)
Long Sutton meeting house
from the graveyard.

Fig 3.10
The exterior of North
Walsham meeting house.

Fig 3.11
The interior of North
Walsham meeting house,
showing the open lobby
and gallery.

ministers' stand raised one step across the rear wall with a panelled
back and a simple double-railed barrier, below which are three benches,
access to the stand being in two places. Both the entrance passage and
the gallery are closed off from the meeting room by timber panelling
incorporating moveable shutters.

Both Long Sutton and Stafford have retained the asymmetric placing
of the entrance in the long wall of a rectangular plan. Our next three
examples adopt a central entrance in an almost square-plan building,
which gives them a much more decidedly 18th-century character.

The first is found a little way to the north of the Norfolk town of
North Walsham. It was built in 1772 to replace an earlier meeting house
and is on an almost square plan, constructed of red brick with a roof of
blue pantiles. The main elevation is symmetrical and of two storeys with
a central doorway, originally with a pediment above, with 12-paned sash
windows either side and three smaller 6-paned windows under the eaves
above (Fig 3.10).

The double doors open onto a full-width lobby, divided off from
the main meeting room by a fixed bench on both sides. Straight ahead
is the ministers' stand, central on the far wall, with benches either side,
originally at a lower level, and reached by two pairs of steps. In front are
fixed benches for the elders and overseers. Above the lobby is a gallery
with an open plain-boarded front, supported on two columns which rise
above the gallery to support the roof. The gallery is reached by two stairs
at either end of the lobby. It is stepped, has fixed forms as seating and is
divided by a rare central partition (Fig 3.11).

The meeting house in Claverham, Somerset, is a most remarkable
building, both in its adoption of 18th-century style and in its dual purpose
as an almshouse and a meeting house. The structure is based on a
half-H plan with the meeting house in the central section and two-storey
projecting wings on either side, the ground floors of which were designed
as cottage accommodation for widows. It is constructed of limestone
rubble coated with render and limewash with a roof of pantiles.

Fig 3.12
The exterior of Claverham
meeting house, the meeting
house straight ahead and the
almshouse wings either side.

The frontage is very grand, with a tall round-headed central doorway containing panelled double doors. On each side are tall round-headed windows with small-paned timber sashes. Both the door and windows have keystones to the arched stonework. Above the door is a small square window and above that the centre of the front is carried up to form the base for a stone pedestal carrying a sundial with a torch finial. The base is inscribed 'THIS HOUSE REBUILT IN THE YEAR 1729'. More remarkably still, this 'frontage' does not face the road but is at right angles to it and virtually hidden away (Fig 3.12).

The meeting house interior is much simpler. Entering through the main door the raised stand is straight ahead beneath a square 15-paned sash window. The ministers' bench is backed by a panelled dado and fronted by a simple rail with a fixed bench beneath it. On both sides the walls are panelled at ground-floor level with piers supporting the upper floor: there were originally open galleries above. On the right-hand side the gallery handrail survives, although the space behind has been walled off; on the left-hand side the gallery became the women's meeting room in 1755 and shutters were put in place to allow it to be opened if necessary. A similar layout with side galleries is also the final form of the meeting house at Penrith (following restructuring in 1803).

Perhaps the grandest meeting house built by Friends around this time was that known as the Friars in Bristol, the city with the largest population of Quakers in the country. In 1669 Quakers had bought from a Friend a portion of the land which had belonged to the Dominican order before the Reformation. A meeting house was built the next year, as described on page 25, which by 1747 had become too small and in need of repair, so the decision was made to rebuild. The design of the new meeting house was entrusted to Quaker builders George Tully and his son William.

They replicated the general form of the old meeting house and built a large square building of two storeys rendered with limewash and with limestone dressings. The front elevation is of three bays with a central

doorcase having a triple-keyed, moulded architrave with pediment above. The two lower windows and the three larger upper ones all have segmental-arched surrounds with sill blocks. The sides are of four bays with similar windows. The walls ascend to a parapet which curves elegantly upwards to the corners and all but hides the large central lantern which arises from the complex slated roof (Fig 3.13).

The interior has large Doric columns on octagonal bases which hold up both the roof and the gallery which is on three sides of the room and is approached by two stairs partially cut into the structure of the walls. The galleries were stepped and had fixed benches, some of which survive. The ministers' stand, which filled the end wall, is no longer present: it was on three levels, the highest of which was 2.5ft (0.75m) above the floor. The central lantern was designed to admit both light and air to the room, ventilation being controlled by a sliding shutter.

The lantern, columns and galleries are elements shared with the nearby Methodist New Room, a much smaller building which had been built for John Wesley in 1739, possibly also by George Tully. The architectural pretensions of the meeting house were criticised by some Friends. Two years later, a visiting Irish Friend remarked that it 'wou'd do as well to have less moulding, cornices etc. which probably cost a good deal'.[4] Nevertheless, a century later it had come to be seen by a Bristol Friend as being 'a good specimen of chastened and correct taste'.[5]

The building was finally abandoned by Quakers in 1954 and sold to the city, which inserted offices within the central meeting room. In 2009 these were removed; it was sensitively restored and has since served as restaurant premises.

Quaker communities

Three country meeting houses from the north are worth introducing at this point because of the light that they cast on the social and other

Fig 3.14
Pardshaw meeting house –
the men's meeting house from
the graveyard, the stable
block beyond.

Fig 3.15
Pardshaw meeting house –
the schoolhouse and entrance
from the lane.

activities of self-sufficient Quaker communities in the 18th century. The earliest is at Pardshaw in Cumbria, where Friends, who had been meeting, initially in the open air, since the 1650s, built their first meeting house in 1672. Fifty years later they began to think of building a new one by purchasing a new site, and in 1729 built their new meeting house, taking care to reuse all that they could from the old. The new building is on a L-shaped plan and contains two meeting houses, built in sandstone rubble with dressed stone details and lime-washed; the roofs are of slate (Fig 3.14). The main meeting room is on the left as you approach from the road and the smaller women's meeting room is to the right. Both are now entered by a porch, built in 1740, and both have hearths and chimneys, as befits the exposed north- and east-facing site. The hearth in the women's meeting room is in the centre of the ministers' stand, a uniquely Cumbrian arrangement.[6] Facing it, and forming the side wall of the main meeting room, for the two are arranged at right angles to each other, is a large panelled screen containing double shutters, the top ones hingeing upwards to be secured from hooks in the ceiling, the lower ones hingeing downwards.

It is not only the meeting houses that are of interest here but the whole of the complex of buildings. Alongside the road was added in 1731 a small stable, later enlarged to cater perhaps for 12 or more horses. Stables were one of the earliest additions to many meeting houses, but this remote example is a rare survival.

A school was soon meeting in the women's meeting house, for education independent of the established church was important to Quakers, and this gained its own schoolroom, alongside the stables, in 1745. It was this school that John Dalton (1766–1844), the scientist, from neighbouring Eaglesfield, attended for his early education. These buildings within their stout perimeter wall, enclosing, as well, the extensive burial ground, were for 200 years the centre of this scattered rural Quaker community (Fig 3.15).

The remains of another Quaker community can be seen in Yorkshire close to the road from Huddersfield to Sheffield. This area of High Flatts is known as Quaker Bottom and lies in a hollow to the east of the main road from which it is reached by a steeply sloping lane. A hamlet of 18th- and 19th-century buildings around a small square, it has been home to a Quaker meeting since 1678. This originally met in a barn which was subsequently converted to a meeting house in 1697 and substantially rebuilt in 1754. The present frontage with its porch and large windows is a result of 19th-century alterations (Fig 3.16).

The interior, however, is almost entirely 18th century, with a full-width ministers' stand on two levels, the benches having panelled backs and a substantial half-panelled rail in front. The gallery, with its panelled and shuttered front, extends over about a third of the meeting room and is supported on cast iron columns. There is a central wrought iron candelabra hanging from the ceiling (Fig 3.17).

The garden at the front of the meeting house was initially the burial ground, but in 1790 it was extended to the rear and gradually grew in size through the 19th century. Originally nearly all the residents were Quaker, there being some families, the Dickinsons and the Woods, with a long association with the community, which supported a Quaker school and other charitable institutions.

Fig 3.16
The exterior of High Flatts meeting house.

Fig 3.17
The interior of High Flatts meeting house.

We have seen Quaker schools associated with meetings before at Brigflatts and Pardshaw. These local institutions were widespread from the first as dissenters were excluded from the grammar schools. George Fox encouraged education in all that was 'civil and useful in the creation',[7] and he and others devised schemes of education and published primers suitable for Quaker children. Some Quaker schools did make arrangements for boarders, but it was not until the end of the 18th century that national Quaker boarding schools were founded, the first being that at Ackworth, near Pontefract (*see* pages 74–5).

As we have seen, up to this point a separate area or room within a meeting house is not always set aside for use as a women's meeting room. It should perhaps be stressed that Quaker women and men were not separated for worship but only for business meetings. It seems to have been often the case that women and men did not meet separately for business in their local meetings, but only when they got together in the wider area for monthly meetings. So it was only those meetings which hosted the monthly meeting which needed to provide a women's meeting room.

It is curious, therefore, that the only meeting house ever built just for the monthly business meeting was built without a women's meeting room. This unique meeting house is at Rookhow in Cumbria on the southern edge of the Grizedale Forest, and was built for the use of what was then Swarthmoor Monthly Meeting, comprising the meetings at Swarthmoor, Cartmel Height and Colthouse (*see* pages 21–3). As everyone had to travel some distance to reach the meeting house, it was supplied with stables, which included a room for servants, and later a gig house for small carriages.

Rookhow was built in 1725 of local stone under a slate roof and is finished in roughcast render. The plan is a T shape with a large gabled two-storey central porch approached by five steps and, in the arms of the T, to the left the full-height meeting house, lit by two 40-paned sash windows, and to the right the caretaker's two-storey cottage (Fig 3.18). The meeting room, 21ft (6.5m) by 40ft (12m), has a balustraded gallery reached by a stair from the porch and a full-width ministers' stand at the other end with panelled dado behind, approached by three steps. The original fitted benches have been removed and the gallery is now boarded off.

Fig 3.18
Rookhow meeting house.

The external view, with its carriage drive and the flanking buildings, gives some idea of the quiet confidence with which these 18th-century inheritors of the tradition of George Fox and Margaret Fell, who lived at Swarthmoor, went about their business. But there remains the mystery of where the women met, although Butler suggests that they might have used the ample cottage kitchen.[8]

Structures designed for larger gatherings

One consequence of Quakers meeting together from across a wider area deserves a comment here. As well as monthly meetings, quarterly meetings, initially for each county, and the annual sessions of London Yearly Meeting which were held at Whitsuntide, there were also yearly meetings for selected areas of the country held at other times of the year. These were generally in areas remote from the capital, for instance, the West Country and Wales. That for the northern counties, which comprised meetings in Cheshire, Lancashire, Cumberland and Westmorland, met annually in April from 1698 to 1798. This was a circulating meeting in that it did not meet at the same place each year. However, it did attract large numbers of Quakers and also the curious from the local region – there were always public meetings as a form of missionary activity.

Sometimes the local meeting house was large enough, or could be temporarily extended, to hold the numbers expected. As noted on page 28 prior to the meeting at Lancaster in 1708, the meeting house was demolished and rebuilt to satisfy the needs of the Yearly Meeting, and alterations are known to have taken place at Carlisle and Kendal for a similar purpose. The meeting was held at Chester in 1717, 1723 and 1739 in a large hall in the town known as the Tennis Court and, on the last occasion, temporary galleries were erected to hold some of those attending, part of which collapsed from the weight of the crowd, but mercifully without injury.

In the end, the routine solution became to erect a temporary structure of wood and cloth called a booth, stand or shape on a convenient piece of land. These were substantial structures capable of holding 1,000–2,000 people, sitting on simple forms. A plan has been preserved of that erected at Blackburn in 1786: this was 84ft (25.5m) long and 78ft (24m) wide and had at the front a ministers' stand occupying the whole width and raised 4ft (1.2m) above the floor, with five rows of seats behind the front rail and two more rows of seats in front. The auditorium had two side aisles with, in between, 34 forms, 51ft (15.5m) long and 2ft (0.6m) apart, facing forward and, at the side, two banks each of 5 forms facing inwards. There were three separate roofs running the length of the booth with gulleys between them and supported on a series of nine posts on each side (Fig 3.19).

This outdoor temporary meeting house had cost about £70 and yet was not large enough for the afternoon public meeting. A Quaker attending reported that there were 'many hundreds that could not get in' so that some of the walls were taken down and 'people stood without as far as I could see'.[9] The ambition of this structure was clearly justified by

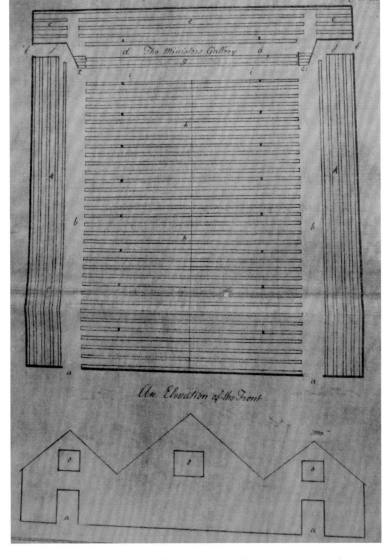

The Ministers Gallery

An Elevation of the Front

Fig 3.19
Plan and elevation of
temporary booth erected for
the Northern Yearly Meeting
at Blackburn in 1786.

the response, but it paints a different picture of 18th-century Quakerism
to that evoked by the dwindling numbers and silent meetings which are
generally thought typical.

Large attendances could also be expected at London Yearly Meeting,
which was held until 1793 at the Gracechurch Street meeting house in
White Hart Court off Lombard Street. Before 1774 this was the original
meeting house built after the Fire of London in 1668, but in that year a
new meeting house was constructed in the very confined space available.
It had a large rooflight and a gallery on two sides supported on Doric
columns. This is the subject of an oil painting of a meeting for worship – a
rare instance for the 18th century. It gives an exaggerated impression
of the width of the room but clearly shows the men and women seated
separately, wearing their hats with the exception of the Friend speaking

from the ministers' stand who has removed his and hung it on the peg behind him (Fig 3.20).

However, by the 1790s Gracechurch Street was becoming too small and, in addition, a separate Women's Yearly Meeting had been instituted in 1784 which could not be accommodated there. So it was agreed to build two new large meeting houses at Devonshire House, a property off Bishopsgate, which Friends had also used since the Great Fire. These were designed by John Bevans, a Quaker architect, and completed in 1793 and 1794 respectively. They were of a horseshoe-shaped plan with entrances in the curved end and the ministers' stand on the end wall, with a sounding board above it; there was a curved gallery occupying all but the end wall. Each held in excess of 1,000 people.

Suburban meeting houses

The late 18th and early 19th centuries were characterised in London by a move from the city, where many Friends had lived and worked since the early days, to the neighbouring suburbs. New larger meeting houses were built towards the end of the 18th century at Deptford, Hammersmith, Ratcliff, Southwark, Spitalfields (known as The Peel), Uxbridge and at Westminster: none of these survive unchanged. Those which do and give us some idea of a suburban London meeting house of this period are Brentford & Isleworth (1785), Wandsworth (1778) and Winchmore Hill (1791).

Wandsworth meeting house retains its sense of being hidden away from the world, which was shared by many London meeting houses of the period. It was built behind a Georgian house on Wandsworth High Street on the site of the burial ground which Friends had been using since the 1670s. An alleyway led through from the street (subsequently roofed in as a lobby and now fronted with a neo-Georgian extension of the 1920s) and the meeting house built at right angles to this (Fig 3.21). It is a single-storey building of square plan in brown brick rising to a parapet with a stone coping which hides the double-hipped tiled roof. The three windows which face south, overlooking the burial ground, have segmental brick arches and are 12-paned sashes.

The main meeting room is dado panelled on all sides, rising up towards the central two-level ministers' stand at the west end, which retains its original doors (Fig 3.22). There is a raised platform around the other three walls, which originally had fixed benches. The women's meeting room is on the north side, separated by a solid wall with a single connecting door. This was built after the main meeting room, filling a courtyard between the meeting room and the house on the High Street, and is lit by high-level windows to the north and east. It too has dado-panelled walls but no remaining fitted furniture.

Brentford & Isleworth meeting house is also secluded by being on a lane, leading away from what was then the main Bath road, and which probably ran through market gardens and now is surrounded by schools

Fig 3.21
Wandsworth meeting house – passageway leading to the burial ground.

Fig 3.22
Wandsworth meeting house – the main meeting room.

and their playing fields. The main frontage faces the lane and has the typical long-wall form of an off-centre entrance with small windows at ground- and first-floor levels on one side and three large window openings on the other. The structure is of brown brick under a slate roof with gable ends which rise from Bath stone corbels. The entrance contains double doors and has a stone hood above on brackets inscribed '11 4 Mo 1785' (ie 11th of the fourth month [April] 1785). On the ground floor is a square window; the other window openings all have brick arches, the peculiarity here being that many of the openings are blind. All the glazed windows have sashes and wooden shutters. This elevation suffered from bomb damage in the 1940s and was reconstructed to the original plans. The back wall contains the same three tall window openings, but all in this case are glazed with sashes and provide the main source of light for the meeting room (Fig 3.23).

The entrance leads into a lobby which contained a fireplace and a stair leading up to a gallery on the first floor. From the lobby, double doors lead into the square meeting room, which is dado panelled on all walls, sweeping up towards the raised ministers' stand, which occupies the whole north gable wall: this is approached by two sets of three steps set a little away from the side walls and whose panelled sides enclose the front bench of the stand. There are fixed benches remaining round three of the walls. At high level on the south side, full-width vertically sliding shutters communicate with the gallery.

Around the meeting house is a large burial ground which, after the closure of metropolitan burial grounds in the 1830s, served for the whole of the west London area and thus contains a large number of burials marked with gravestones (permitted again for Quakers in 1850).

Winchmore Hill meeting house also has a large burial ground which dates back to 1682, but which was enlarged in 1821 to take burials from other London meetings. The wall surrounding it is marked with small square alphabetically inscribed stones laying out the grid on which the burials were arranged, a rare survival. The meeting house itself is thought to have been designed, like those at Devonshire House, by John Bevans and, in contrast to Brentford & Isleworth, is of the gable-end type and built of stock brick with a slate roof (Fig 3.24). The entrance front is of three bays with a central entrance under a stone hood on stone brackets,

Fig 3.23 (below left)
Brentford meeting house.

Fig 3.24 (below right)
Winchmore Hill meeting house.

flanked by a pair of straight-headed sash windows with external shutters. Above this is a simple pediment with a blind circular recess, giving a nod to Classical taste. Each of the side walls has a single sash window. Inside, very little remains of the original furnishings except for the dado panelling and fixed benches on three of the walls.

The move to the suburbs also occurred in Bristol, if a little later. Stimulated by the move of Joseph Storrs Fry, the chocolate manufacturer, to Frenchay village in 1801, the old meeting house on Frenchay common was rebuilt in 1809. The meeting house stands, similarly to Wandsworth, a little way back from the road and parallel to it, on the edge of the burial ground. Fronting the road were originally a coach house and stables facing each other across a yard. The present frontage dates from 1815, when a new women's meeting house was built over the coach house, thus roofing in the passage through to the main meeting house. This acquired an arched entrance way, matched by another leading into the yard between the former coach house and what is now a cottage. The walls are of rubble stone with a covering of limewash and the two semi-circular arched windows of the upper meeting room have sashes and external shutters. These, together with the pantiled hipped roof and the yellow ochre of the limewash, give the whole a domestic and vaguely Mediterranean flavour (Fig 3.25).

Inside, the flagged passageway which leads to the burial ground has off it a narrow stairway leading to the upper women's meeting room and then double doors which give onto a vestibule to the main meeting room, with stairs on the left leading up to the loft or gallery. A full-height timber screen separates the vestibule and the loft space above from the main meeting room, incorporating sliding panels to enable these areas to be included in the main room (Fig 3.26). This room is a well-proportioned double-height space with a coved ceiling and dado panelling round the walls, lit by two large semi-circular arched windows straight ahead and to the left. There is a blocked matching window to the right obscured by the building of the upper meeting room. The original ministers' stand with ramped dado has been retained, three steps above floor level, and

Fig 3.25
The exterior of Frenchay meeting house.

Fig 3.26
Frenchay meeting house interior – the screen.

there are fixed seats round two of the walls raised up a single step, as at Wandsworth.

The gallery, which extends over both the vestibule and the passageway, was initially intended to be sufficient for the women's business meeting. That this was not the case is illustrated by the dimensions of the 1815 upper meeting room, which match those of the main meeting room in all except height. It too has fixed benches round three of the sides, raised a single step. It also perhaps serves to demonstrate the growing confidence of Quaker women in the importance of their role in the Society.

The 18th-century meeting house

Although modestly proportioned meeting houses continued to be built throughout the 18th century, the trend was for building and rebuilding more substantial structures. The long-wall meeting house with asymmetrically placed entrance was slowly replaced as a model and more symmetrical designs and Classical features, which had begun to be seen at the end of the 17th century, became commonplace.

In line with the increased reliance on recorded ministers in the meeting for worship and the increase in the formal discipline, the ministers' stand became a more dominant feature of meeting rooms, invariably occupying the whole of one wall and having more than one level to provide for the seating of elders and overseers. The small stand with room for only three or four, as at Wallingford, was confined to the past.

The other change was the increasing importance of the women's meeting room in the design of meeting houses. The provision of a substantially sized room, whether it could be opened up into the men's meeting room by means of shutters, as at Pardshaw, or was entirely separate, as at Wandsworth or Frenchay, became a necessity for any meeting which wanted to maintain a leading role in Quaker affairs. This was a reflection of the development in society as a whole of a separate sphere of action for women, particularly in the middle class, to which Quakers increasingly belonged.

An American postscript

Eighteenth-century American Quakers were much affected by the onset of the Revolutionary War (1775–83), suffering harassment in some places for refusing to fight and losing members who chose to take up arms. Some Philadelphia Quakers who had been disowned for failure to uphold the peace testimony set up the Religious Society of Free Quakers in 1780, and in 1783 built their own meeting house which still stands in Philadelphia, although not on its original site.

This is an elegant building of three bays with a central pedimented entrance with five 20-paned sash windows on the entrance front, which is flanked by brick pilasters (Fig 3.27). The meeting room was originally of full height, but in 1788 the building was divided into two floors for easier letting of the rooms. It also had at least two cellars, which were also let.

Fig 3.27
Free Quakers meeting house,
Philadelphia.

One group of American Quakers who were particularly affected by refusing to join the conflict were the Quaker whalers of Nantucket Island in Massachusetts. In 1792 about 50 of them accepted an invitation from the agent of Sir William Hamilton to form a whaling colony in Milford Haven, Pembrokeshire, which he was developing as a major Atlantic port. Initially they joined for worship with the surviving Welsh Friends in the area, acquiring a site of their own in the town for a burial ground in 1801. Eventually they employed a local architect, Griffith Watkins, to build a meeting house on part of the burial ground, which finally opened in 1811, described by one of their number as a 'snug neet thing'.[10]

Milford Haven meeting house is a modest structure, rectangular on plan, with rendered walls and a hipped slate roof. The front elevation is dominated by a central projecting two-storey porch with a gabled slate roof. Above the doorway is a 6-paned arched window and to either side of the porch are 24-paned windows lighting the meeting rooms (Fig 3.28). The porch has doors to both meeting rooms, the men's to the right and the women's to the left. However, these are not side by side, with the ministers' stand on the long wall, as would have been the American pattern, but the ministers' stand is in the men's room across the short wall. The women's meeting room had a fireplace, and the rooms were separated by a partition with moveable shutters: the present partition is of a later date. The ministers' stand is original, panelled front and back and with central balustraded steps (Fig 3.29).

The meeting house has been extended twice in the last 50 years to give more flexible spaces for meeting and community use: eight of the old slate gravestones have been affixed to the rear wall. They have unusual canted or concave corners and record only the initials of the deceased, the year and the month of death. Dated between 1801 and 1829, well before Quaker gravestones were permitted in Britain, they continue to bear a witness to independence of spirit of the founders of this extraordinary American colony (Fig 3.30).

Notes

1   This is a Biblical phrase used by a number of the Jewish prophets to describe the faithful who will be spared God's punishment of the nation of Israel (associated with the Babylonian and Assyrian invasions). It is taken up by Paul in Romans to illustrate God's grace in sparing the true believers in a sinful world.

2   Boswell, J 1791 *Life of Johnson*. Boswell records that on Sunday 31 July 1763 he visited a Quaker meeting and heard a woman preach. Despite Johnson's typically robust rejoinder, he was acquainted with a number of Quakers, both men and women. As a staunch Anglican, he disapproved strongly of Quaker missionary activities.

3   Watts 1995, 336, quoting conclusions from Pratt, D H 1985 *Quakers and the First Industrial Revolution*.

4   This was John Lecky of Cork (1764–1838) in a manuscript diary transcribed as 'An Irishman at London Yearly Meeting in 1794', see Anon 1918, 4.

5   This was William Tanner (1815–66) in his *Three Lectures on the Early History of the Society of Friends in Bristol and Somersetshire*.

6   See Butler 1999a, 900.

7   Nickalls 1952, 520.

8   Butler 1999a, 336.

9   Cooksey 2011.

10 Quaker Meeting Houses Heritage Project (2016) *Friends Meeting House, Milford Haven* at heritage.quaker.org.uk/files/Milford Haven LM.pdf, quoting the diary of Abial Folger (1736–1816) for 1 March 1811.

4 A turbulent century

Quaker buildings 1815–1915

Two historical movements which began in the 18th century made the major impacts on Quakerism in the 19th century: the Industrial Revolution and the evangelical revival. The rise of Quaker entrepreneurs continued from the previous century. Quaker simplicity had never involved eschewing individual wealth, providing it was used responsibly by promoting good works and not living too ostentatiously. The 19th century saw the rise of further Quaker dynasties onto the national scene, including Clarks of Street, shoe manufacturers (1825); Horniman, tea merchants (1820s); Pease of Darlington, railways and mining (1820s); and Reckitt of Hull, household good suppliers (1840). By the mid-century the proportion of the very rich among Quakers was some fifty-fold greater than their proportion in the population.[1]

With business success had come involvement in the world and in municipal affairs, particularly in the growing industrial cities without royal charters, where the restrictions of the Test Acts did not apply. Further opportunities arose on the repeal of the Test Acts in 1828. Joseph Pease, the son of the founder of the Stockton & Darlington Railway (1825), became the first Quaker to enter Parliament in 1832. Successful Quakers began to shake off the constraints of the Society's rules and become what were known as 'gay' Quakers. They wanted their religious affiliation to be as acceptable in wider society as that of other dissenters.

The most important change in the religious landscape of the 18th century had been the rise of Methodism, which, in its emphasis on public preaching and evangelisation, had shared many features with early Quakerism. The Methodist movement grew from a ginger group within the Anglican church to a denomination with some 10,000 English congregations by the mid-19th century. This in turn evoked an evangelical revival within the other denominations with an insistence on Bible study and the importance of recognising Christ as a personal saviour.

Eighteenth-century Quakerism had, in general, thought of the Bible as secondary in importance to the Inward Light, and Bible reading was not encouraged. However, the increasing interaction with the world and, in particular, the Quaker involvement with the movement for the abolition of the slave trade brought Friends into contact with the more progressive Anglican evangelicals, such as Wilberforce and Clarkson. There is a recognisable increase in biblical language in Yearly Meeting epistles from the end of the 18th century, reflecting an increased interest in evangelicalism within the Society. Indeed, Quakers were in at the founding of the British & Foreign Bible Society in 1804. There followed a struggle within the Society between the evangelically minded, largely urban, Friends and the mostly rural 'conservative' Friends, who gave primacy to the Inward Light, which lasted for the first part of the 19th century.

In the newly independent United States this led to major splits among Quakers which lasted for the next century (in Philadelphia from 1827 to 1955). British Friends came to a typical compromise in which evangelical piety came to dominate Quaker religious behaviour, while the non-scriptural concept of the Inward Light was never denied. The 1850s and 1860s also saw a number of changes which made Friends much less of a 'peculiar people' – disownment for marrying a non-Quaker was abolished, wedding rings were permitted, the rules around dress were relaxed, and gravestones were permitted in burial grounds. Yet many still left to join other denominations, some playing a major part in the founding of a new Nonconformist group, the Brethren. At the 1851 religious census, Quaker numbers had fallen to the low point of around 17,000 members in 363 meetings, only 0.1 per cent of the population. This decrease led to closure of a number of meeting houses for shorter or longer periods during the 19th century. The buildings usually found other purposes, which have left their impact on the internal furnishings of many a meeting house subsequently brought back into use.

However, just as the evangelicals gained the upper hand, the seeds of a subsequent reversal of fortunes were being sown. Evangelical Quakers became leaders in the adult school movement, inaugurated First-day (or Sunday) schools for both adults and children, and started mission services for working people. They also looked after young Quakers drawn away from home to work in the growing cities by forming institutes for fellowship and self-education.

The opening of the universities to dissenters from the 1850s had also led to a wider education for young Quakers. It was particularly well-educated Friends associated with the thriving institute in Manchester who led the way in demanding that Quakerism responded to modern ideas but also return to its historic roots, leading to the eventual triumph of liberal theology among British Quakers in the 20th century.

Large urban meeting houses

In 1817 York Quakers opened a new large meeting house, their third on the site that they still occupy in Friargate, not far from the castle. The architects, Watson and Pritchett of York, designed a generously proportioned building in the Classical style but with little external ornament. The frontage was of five bays with blind window recesses at two levels topped by a pediment. There were three entrances from a portico which led into a central lobby with stone steps up to the gallery level (Fig 4.1). The main meeting room beyond was of a considerable size, being 57ft (17m) long, 46ft (14m) wide and 27ft (8m) high. The stand occupied the whole of the facing wall; the room was galleried on three sides and lit by 13 large windows positioned just below the ceiling and 2 smaller windows in the ground floor either side of the stand. This room was capable of seating 1,200 people (Fig 4.2).

The women's meeting room was modified from part of the previous building and was not rebuilt until further changes were made in 1885. The 1817 building also boasted a library, a strong room and men's and women's toilet blocks on either side of the central yard (Fig 4.3). There was also the very latest in warm-air heating and ventilation, although the room was lit at night by six chandeliers. The total cost was £3,274, at least £3 million in 2021 money.

The reason we know so much about this particular building project is that a member of the meeting, and indeed of the committee which organised the project, the printer and bookseller William Alexander (1768–1841), published three years later his *Observations on the Construction and Fitting up of Meeting Houses … Including One Lately Erected in the City of York*. It contains an exhaustive description of the new meeting house, complete with plans, and hymns its superiority over the recently built Yearly Meeting Houses in London. It is also notable for being the first of a series of books, written by members of different Nonconformist denominations and published during the 19th century, to advise their coreligionists on the best way to build a meeting house or chapel for what was to be the biggest boom in the construction of religious buildings in the nation's history.

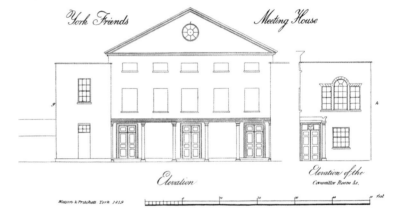

Fig 4.1
The front elevation of the York meeting house of 1817 from the original drawings of Watson & Pritchett, as reproduced in Alexander (1820).

Fig 4.2
Interior of the men's meeting room at York meeting house (1817) photographed in 1957 before demolition. Note the sounding board over the ministers' stand.

York Quakers typified this trend and were undoubtedly eager to show their fellow citizens that they could own places of worship every bit as tasteful and elegant as those of other denominations. Yet the membership of York Monthly Meeting, which contained a number of other meeting houses, was only 155 in 1820 and, even with the addition of children, servants and other adherents, a meeting house of this size can only have been justified for the holding of large occasions such as Yorkshire Quarterly Meeting. On census Sunday, 30 March 1851, when membership had grown, the largest attendance was only 273.

The previous year, Friends in Kendal, a town where perhaps 10 per cent of the townsfolk were Quaker, had rebuilt their sizeable 18th-century meeting house to designs by a local architect, Francis Webster, with a meeting room which held 850, for £3,637. The external appearance lacked the explicit classicism of that at York, but it was judged 'a plain substantial and most respectable looking building' by a visiting Quaker.[2]

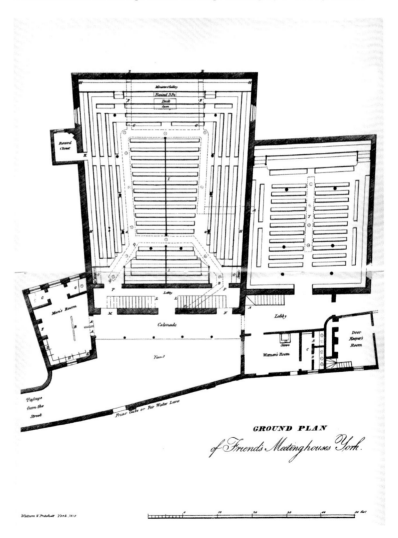

Fig 4.3
Plan drawing of York meeting house as it existed in 1817, taken from the original plans. The women's meeting house was not new built at that time but was adapted from one of the previous buildings, as reproduced in Alexander (1820).

GROUND PLAN
of Friends Meetinghouses York.

The two-storey building is faced with hammer-dressed local limestone and roofed in slate. The main southern aspect, which faces the river across the burial ground, is of five bays with a square porch on the right and four semi-circular-headed sash windows to the left (Fig 4.4). The first floor has short eight-paned sashes illuminating the gallery level. A long lobby runs south to north from the porch to a northern entrance facing Stramongate. The large and small meeting houses are set at right angles to this axis and are, as at York, placed side by side. However, here there was a wooden screen between the two rooms of four arched openings incorporating structural columns. These contained sliding sashes which could be lowered into the cellar by winches in the attic, thus creating one large room.

The meeting rooms each had a curved gallery on two sides, partly extending over the lobby, and the three-tiered ministers' stand was continued across both meeting houses at the far end, a design more familiar in America (Fig 4.5). Above the stand sat large elegant tripartite sash windows.

This meeting house has, since 1994, housed the Quaker Tapestry exhibition in the large meeting room, whereas the small meeting room has undergone considerable 20th-century modification to become the main place for meeting for worship, with classrooms above.

Another centre of Quakerism since the early years is Norwich where, in 1826, a thriving meeting, prominent among which were the Gurneys of Earlham Hall, decided to rebuild its city-centre meeting house on Goat Lane, which had survived with much alteration since 1679. Building on a restricted site with a very narrow street frontage, a local architect, Thomas Patience, skilfully designed a substantial building which presented to the city a Classical face, imparting an air of substantial respectability.

From the street you enter a small courtyard enclosed with iron railings with two-storey wings on either side and are presented with a flight of steps up to a massive porch of yellowish stone with four unfluted Doric columns, framing double doors (Fig 4.6). There are no windows at ground-floor level, but above the porch are three large round-headed windows separated by pilasters topped with a plain entablature and cornice. The whole is in a greyish brick with stone dressings. The two wings are not symmetrical, the one on the right being intended as a caretaker's cottage and that on the left as a cloakroom block.

At the rear of the building, which is in red brick, are three similar round-headed windows in rectangular recesses with a stone lintel which light the women's meeting house. This is set, unusually, behind the main meeting house and at right angles to it. The side walls of the structure are again in red brick, with the same recessed round-headed windows, some of which are blind.

Inside the main doors is a lobby with two stairways to gallery level, leading to a draught lobby, on either side of which were two small rooms, one a library. Two double doors lead from this into the main meeting room, about 40ft (12m) square with a two-tiered ministers' stand at the far end, and on each side wall benches raised a single step (Fig 4.7). There is a rear gallery over the lobbies, now boarded up and converted to meeting rooms. This is apparently supported on four wooden Ionic columns.

Fig 4.4
Kendal meeting house from
the south.

Fig 4.5
The interior of the men's
meeting room at Kendal
meeting house, looking
through one of the open
shutters into part of the
women's meeting room.
[Drawing by David Butler]

Fig 4.6
Goat Lane meeting house, Norwich – entrance front showing the two wings flanking the courtyard and the grand porch.

Fig 4.7
Interior of the main meeting room at Goat Lane, Norwich. Note the fixed benches along the sides and the ministers' stand at the far end extending the full width of the meeting house.

The women's meeting house, 40ft (12m) long by 25ft (7.5m) wide has a similar gallery, still extant, with stepped flooring. It apparently never had a ministers' stand but has wall seats on a raised step round all three sides.

Manchester Quakers were a larger body than Quakers in the other towns and cities we have so far considered and had moved in 1795 to a site on Mount Street near to the newly developing St Peter's Square. However, in a little over 30 years this meeting house was found to be insufficient and in 1828 the decision was made to demolish and rebuild on the same site, initially with seating for 600 on the ground floor. A local Quaker architect, Richard Lane, was given the job and he designed a meeting house in the Classical style using as a model one of the temples illustrated in *The Antiquities of Athens* by James Stuart and Nicholas Revett (1762–1816) – an influential sourcebook for the Greek Revival (Fig 4.8).

The building itself is rectangular, of two storeys over a basement, and is built in red brick with stone dressings. The entrance front on Mount Street, however, is entirely of stone, of five bays with giant pilasters at the corners and a central portico with four embedded Ionic columns supporting a frieze inscribed 'FRIEND'S MEETING HOUSE', with a pediment above. Although the original entrance had three double doors, only the central one remains, the others having become windows, which are in general 12-paned sashes. The side elevations are of ten bays with 12-paned sash windows to both floors.

Inside, the main meeting room, 58ft (18m) square, occupied the rear half of the building. It had raised seats on two sides with a gallery above supported on fluted Doric columns. The two-tiered ministers' stand, slightly curved, occupied the far end with a sounding board above. It was approached from the front lobby by two wide corridors on either side of the building, in the centre of which was the smaller women's meeting room, similarly fitted up and with galleries which continued those in the main meeting room. The partition between the two rooms was moveable, half sinking into the floor and the other half rising into the roof to unite the two into a single room, described in 1845 by *The British Friend*[3] as 'majestic … of singular elegance and dignified simplicity' (Fig 4.9). Although the whole may have been capable of holding up to 1,900 people,

Fig 4.8
Friends meeting house, Mount Street, Manchester. This engraving published in Lancashire Illustrated *(1831) shows the original design with triple doorways under the portico.*
[From a print in the possession of the author]

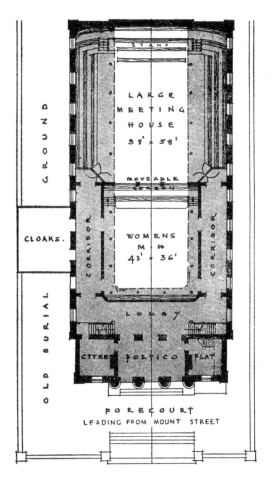

Fig 4.9
Plan drawing of Manchester meeting house as built in 1830 taken from the original plans. Shaded areas represent the presence of a second storey. Note the corridors either side of the women's meeting room for access to the men's meeting room.
[Drawing by Hubert Lidbetter]

the majority of those seats were in the gallery, the number of seats on the floor being sufficient for the day-to-day needs of the Quaker community.

This phenomenon of the large urban meeting house was not restricted to these towns and cities. During the century substantial new meeting houses were also built in Birmingham (1857), Bradford (1878) and Leeds (1868), of which only the last survives, with changed use as a university building (Fig 4.10). Just why these prosperous urban Quakers were so keen on building meeting houses of such a size is hard to gauge. As mentioned above, there was an element of 'keeping up with the Joneses' in relation to other Nonconformist groups. However, prominent among the proponents of these larger meeting houses were evangelical Quakers such as, in Norwich, Joseph John Gurney (1788–1847) and, in Manchester, Isaac Crewdson (1780–1844). They may have been looking to a future in which Friends would attract much larger numbers of worshippers – more of a policy of 'build it and they will come'. That eventuality was not to be, and so these buildings have only survived into the 21st century in considerably modified form.

Quakers and their architects

Unlike most earlier meeting houses, which were built and designed by the members of the meeting themselves or by a local builder, these large urban meeting houses were typically architect-designed. Designers of earlier buildings, such as the Tullys in Bristol, were often building contractors first and foremost. John Bevans (1743–1809) of Plaistow, who designed the Yearly Meeting Houses at Devonshire House, was such a one. He was a Quaker and all his known works are for Quaker clients: perhaps best known are his designs for The Retreat, the Quaker asylum at York.

Friends had at first been hostile to all the arts, seeing them as 'creaturely' distractions from attention to the Inward Teacher; however, drawing, as an aid to study of the natural world, and devotional forms of writing, including poetry, were often excepted from the general disapproval, particularly if pursued in private. The Quaker attitude to the arts gradually became less negative through the 19th century, and architecture, since it had a practical end in the construction of buildings, as it became a distinct profession, was never apparently censured by Friends.

The first professional Quaker architect was Thomas Rickman (1776–1841) whose *Attempt to Discriminate the Styles of English Architecture* (1817) set out and gave names to the various stages of English medieval architecture by which they are still known. Although a prolific designer of Anglican churches, he never designed a meeting house. Richard Lane (1795–1880), who designed Mount Street, Manchester, was in the 1830s one of Manchester's most prominent architects and was also the architect of the Victoria Park suburb south of the centre of the city. His practice in partnership with P B Alley was the place in which a much more famous Quaker architect trained. This was Alfred Waterhouse (1830–1905), son of a Liverpool Quaker cotton merchant and famed as the architect of Manchester Town Hall and the National History Museum in Kensington. His only Quaker meeting house is that at Cartmel in Cumbria of 1859.

This is, for Waterhouse, an undistinguished building, which could easily be taken from the outside for a small Anglican church of the period were it not for the absence of a chancel or any overt Christian symbolism. It stands back from the road behind a sweeping carriage drive, itself unusual for a Quaker meeting house, and is of four bays with the first containing a gabled porch. It is built of stone covered in roughcast render with limestone dressings and a slate roof. The three tall segmentally arched windows at front and back are separated by stepped buttresses which give a vaguely Gothic feel to the building. Inside, the porch leads to a flagged lobby with a stair to the former gallery on the left and the

Fig 4.11
Cartmel meeting house, designed by Alfred Waterhouse and built in 1859.

double doors to the meeting room on the right. The meeting room is beautifully light and has a two-tiered stand filling the gable wall with dado panelling behind and on the side walls to the level of the sills. There is now a suspended ceiling, whereas the room would originally have been open to the rafters (Fig 4.11).

Quakers also used non-Quaker architects for their buildings, as we have seen above. James Pritchett (1789–1868), part of the practice which designed the 1817 York Meeting House, later designed in 1847 an elegant Classical meeting house at the Quaker school at Ackworth, near Pontefract, used today both by the school and the local Quaker meeting. The school was originally built as the northern site of the Foundling Hospital in 1758–63, which closed in 1773 and was purchased by Friends

Fig 4.12
The meeting house at Ackworth School near Pontefract of 1847, designed by James Pritchett. The colonnade leads round to the school entrance on the left.

Fig 4.13
The interior of the meeting house at Ackworth with the ministers' stand straight ahead. The bench seating on the floor is proportioned for schoolchildren and not for adults.

Fig 4.14
The exterior of Gloucester
meeting house. The original
meeting house of 1835 by
Samuel Daukes can just
be seen to left and right,
but is largely hidden by the
pedimented entrance wing of
1879 and the single-storey
post-war additions either
side.

Fig 4.15
The ministers' stand at
Gloucester. Note the five steps
with decoratively pierced
risers. The bench for the
elders is raised one step above
the floor.

as a boarding school, which commenced in 1779. The meeting house was
originally within the school buildings, but when a separate building was
commissioned it clearly had to match the Palladian style of the existing
buildings. Pritchett's design is rectangular of three by five bays and with
two storeys, built in sandstone. The front contains three double doors
with above them three 12-paned sash windows, topped with a pediment
with a central circular window (Fig 4.12). The entrance doors give onto
a colonnade with Tuscan columns which turns at right angles to link the
meeting house to the main school entrance. Inside is a single large room
of greater than 50ft (15m) wide by 70ft (21m) long with a two-tiered
stand on the opposite gable wall. There is a horseshoe-shaped gallery
on three sides, supported on thin metal columns; the floor is stepped up
under the gallery with fixed benches against the wall (Fig 4.13). Overall,
the similarity to the 1817 meeting house at York is quite striking.

Pritchett had as a pupil Samuel Daukes (1811–80) who, after
designing the buildings for another Quaker school, at Sidcot in Somerset,
was responsible for designing four meeting houses in the 1830s and
1840s. The only one which survives in use is that at Gloucester, built in
1835. It is set back behind a wall in Greyfriars, near the historic centre
of the city, and accessed through a two-storey gatehouse. The original
building is now almost eclipsed from view by an imposing two-storey
addition of 1879 which provided a committee room and classroom, with
larger entrance hall and further single-storey flat-roofed additions of
1946. All of this is in red brick with a hipped roof. Daukes's building had
five round-arched windows high in the long wall facing the street. These
are set in arched brick recesses with darker brick details, a graceful effect.
The 1879 addition is more blatantly Classical, with giant brick pilasters
either side of the doorway rising to support an open pediment with stone
dressings (Fig 4.14). Inside, the original building is in two rooms, three
bays for the men and two for the women, divided by a large wooden sash
shutter, sliding both up and down, and of novel tripartite design, all three
sections with arched tops, the side sections containing communicating
doors. At the other end of the main meeting room is an unusually high
stand, with a flight of five steps at either side, flanked with moulded
handrails, the risers with pierced decoration to encourage ventilation
(Fig 4.15). A wooden dado covers all three walls, raised over the stand
and with fixed benches beneath on the other walls.

Characteristics of the mid-19th-century meeting house

The ordering of the interior of Gloucester meeting house is in many ways typical of Quaker meeting houses of the mid-19th century. A single rectangular high-ceilinged room, with large sash windows high in the long walls, divided asymmetrically in two by wooden shutters is the typical design. The smaller space will be for the women's business meeting and the larger for the men's business meeting. The ministers' stand will be in the larger room on one short (gable) wall, indicating that this would be the space used for regular worship with the shutters raised and/or lowered only for large gatherings.

Arranged on increasingly heavily built benches, the worshippers continued to be divided with women on one side of the room and men on the other, this segregation reflected in the seating on the stand, or as they were also known, the 'facing benches'. This segregation continued until late in the century, slowly giving way to Friends sitting wherever they wished, families sitting together rather than separated.

Stands became more prominent during this period, either, as at Gloucester, by being raised higher or by having three rows of seats as at Warrington (1830). It also became more usual to have some form of sounding board above the stand. Of course, these were, in part, responses to the larger rooms and loftier ceilings, which also required the ministers and elders to see into and to be seen from the back of the room and to be heard throughout these large spaces. However, they went along with increases in the relative importance attached to preaching and prayer over silent waiting in the increasingly evangelical atmosphere of Victorian Quakerism.

More attention can be seen to be given to ventilation and heating in meeting houses – large ceiling roses leading to roof ventilators are frequently present, as less frequently are ventilating outlets in side walls. Sometimes stone or brick squares survive in meeting house floors indicating where a stove (such as that seen in the old photograph of

Fig 4.16
The stables at Gildersome meeting house, between Leeds and Huddersfield, built in 1849 for a meeting house of 1756. Stables were a necessity for country meeting houses if they were to host monthly or quarterly meetings.

Lancaster) originally stood. Reading (1835) retains one curved recessed stove back (of an original four) set into the wall, and at Ross-on-Wye (1805) a small solid-fuel stove was still stored in the meeting house when the author visited in 2019.

Externally, meeting houses were still most likely to have a rectangular ground plan with the entrance on the long wall; designs were more likely to be Classical with rounded arches where present rather than the Gothic, which was rapidly becoming common for other Nonconformists. Tuscan colonnades became more frequent as an element of the entrance front, although porches continued to be built.

Cloakrooms and toilets were built into new meeting houses and added externally, at least for the women, to older buildings. Stables, gig sheds and accommodation for coachmen and other servants were a necessary feature, especially in country areas, although few remain standing, as they do at Brant Broughton, Cartmel, Gildersome (1854) (Fig 4.16) and Rookhow.

At Dorking, Surrey, a new meeting house was built in 1846 which illustrates many of these features. It is of rectangular plan in red brick with a hipped slate roof, having five bays on the long wall facing the street with 12-paned sash windows under flat arches. In front of this is a single-storey flat-roofed porch of three bays with 16-paned sashes either side of a small portico with Tuscan columns (Fig 4.17). The main building is divided asymmetrically as at Gloucester, but this time with a counter-balanced wooden partition under a wide three-centred arch (Fig 4.18). The winding mechanism is still functional: the top half of the partition can be winched into the roof while the bottom half, with its double doors, drops into the floor. The lobby leads straight into the main meeting room.

Reading has a similar three-centred arch near the middle of the room, which originally held the vertical sliding partition which could be winched into the roof. Another similar lies at the rear of the stand, and the wall behind it is coved to act as a sounding board.

The influence of Quaker families

Reading was, of course, home to Huntley and Palmers, biscuit manufacturers, which had in 1835 not yet come to dominate the town. Another Quaker firm which was synonymous with its town was Clarks of Street, shoe manufacturers. Street acquired a new meeting house in 1850, designed by J Francis Cotterell of Bath, an acquaintance of the Clark family. It occupies a site, next to the shoe factory, on which the former meeting house of the 1680s had stood, and making a clear architectural statement of the importance of the family business to the growing town. The new meeting house is at right angles to the road, a handsome building built of the local blue lias ashlar above a rusticated stone base with a hipped slate roof. The main elevation has a projecting Bath stone porch upon three steps with two 20-paned sash windows on the left side and three on the right. On this latter side of the porch there is, partly under the third window, a door which led to the cottage which originally occupied this end bay (now containing schoolrooms). The roof has a large wooden ventilator on the ridge above the meeting room and a chimney stack above the cottage (Fig 4.19).

Fig 4.19
The exterior of Street meeting house, handsomely built in blue lias stone.

Fig 4.20
The sliding sashed shutters at Street, resembling nothing so much as the sliding blackboards once ubiquitous in school classrooms and lecture halls.

Fig 4.21
The Skinnergate frontage
of Darlington meeting
house as rebuilt in 1839/40
and presenting a vaguely
corporate face to the world.

Fig 4.22
The ministers' stand in
the main meeting room at
Darlington (1846), with its
deeply coved sounding board
and gates at either end. The
slightly cramped feeling is
due to the alterations of the
1960s, which divided the
meeting houses to provide
space for commercial letting
by inserting an upper floor
and false ceilings.

Inside the porch, the double doors lead to a wooden draught lobby with openings to the main meeting room and the former women's meeting room. These are separated by a full-height wooden sashed shutter within a rectangular wooden frame (Fig 4.20). Another door, matching the lobby on the other side of the shutter, allows access between the two rooms. Both meeting rooms have dado panelling and fixed benches on the walls; the stand in the main meeting room is only raised on two steps and has a simple rail in front of it with two entrances to either side. The elegant benches in the main meeting room are probably contemporary with the building.

Darlington, in the rapidly developing industrial North East, was home to at least two Quaker dynasties – the Backhouses and the Peases: the Quaker connection is still reflected in the nickname of Darlington Football Club – 'The Quakers'. Friends had worshipped in the centre of the town in Skinnergate since 1678, but the wealth of the members and the growing importance of the town led to rebuilding in a grander style. First, in 1839/40, the buildings on the street front were demolished and replaced with a red brick building of two storeys and five bays which contained lobbies, toilets and committee rooms reached through a porch with Tuscan columns, not unlike that at Dorking (Fig 4.21). A very similar porch was also designed by Samuel Daukes for his meeting house at Staines of 1844, now demolished.

In a second phase, the 18th-century meeting house behind the Skinnergate frontage was demolished in 1846 and rebuilt on the American pattern, as at Kendal, with the men's and women's meeting houses of equal size side by side and separated by sliding sash shutters. Both had galleries at the entrance side, reached by an elegant double staircase from the central lobby, and a ministers' stand up three steps with a large curved sounding board above and a panelled rail at the front. The entrances at either end were guarded by gates (Fig 4.22). Who the architect was for these meeting houses is not clear, but it may have been either Joshua or Joseph Sparkes, both from a Quaker family, the latter the architect for the Stockton & Darlington railway.

Finally, we turn to the market town of Wisbech in the Cambridgeshire fen country, once an important inland port. Here a Quaker grocer, Jonathan Peckover, settled in the late 18th century and thrived, turning to banking, eventually in partnership with Gurney and Co. of Norwich. The house he purchased in the 1790s on the fashionable North Brink, beside the tidal river Nene, still stands and is cared for by the National Trust. In 1854, on a neighbouring plot, a new meeting house was built to replace an older structure. This was to designs by Algernon Peckover, Jonathan's younger son, who was also responsible for designing or improving several other buildings in the town.

The building is stylish, built of yellow gault brick with stone dressings: it is almost square on plan and has four bays along the street front with a mansard roof. The entrance door is at one end with three 12-paned sash windows to its right – all have stone architraves and heavy corbelled hoods. Above the door is inscribed 'FRIENDS MEETING HOUSE', with above that a stone plaque inscribed with the date 1854. Under the rightmost window is another door leading straight into

Fig 4.23
Wisbech meeting house of 1854, facing the river Nene across the North Brink. The main entrance is to the left with the 'coffin door' at the other side. The dormers are not original but part of the 1970s reordering which provided flats for the elderly.

Fig 4.24
The meeting room at Wisbech from the gallery showing the ministers' stand and the curtained off 'coffin door'.

the meeting room. This 'coffin door' was, as its name suggests, for the convenience of undertakers (Fig 4.23).

The original interior plan was a modification of the plan at Darlington, with two meeting houses side by side leading out of a common lobby area and separated by a sashed shutter. A gallery over the lobby served both rooms, the women's room to the rear being about two-thirds the width of the men's room. A reordering took place in 1972, whereby an extra floor was added and the building extended to the rear to provide accommodation for the elderly.

The current meeting room has, as a consequence, a wall where the shutters once stood, a lowered ceiling and modern doors, but the woodwork is mostly original, with a panelled dado, panelled rear and front to the ministers' stand, and a panelled screen dividing off the lobby, the doorway decorated with wooden pilasters. Also, as at Darlington, the entrance to the stand is gated (Fig 4.24).

The variety of 19th-century meeting houses

We have seen two main 19th-century plan types so far, the first in which a large rectangular meeting room with a single ministers' stand is divided unequally into men's and women's meetings rooms (for business meetings) by a large vertical screen of shutters (as at Manchester and Gloucester) and a second in which two similar meeting rooms are built side by side with a shuttered screen on the side wall between them and a stand which extends across both rooms (as at Kendal and Darlington: what I have referred to as the 'American plan'). Another meeting house plan, a variant of the first, was also built in the 19th century. This was first seen at Swarthmoor, where the men's and women's meeting houses are separated by the corridor which leads from the entrance, necessitating two sets of shutters in order to open the two up to each other. In that original case it was caused by building the meeting house as an extension of an existing house, whose downstairs room became the women's meeting house; the later examples were purpose built.

In 1817 the meeting house at Uxbridge was rebuilt along these lines, the third meeting house on this site. It is built of brick on a rectangular plan with a shallow hipped roof of slate. The front is of four bays with three high round-headed sash windows, two lighting the main room and the third the smaller room; the entrance door is off-centre in the third bay. This leads into a lofty corridor built with floor-to-ceiling shutters on both sides. The panelling on the right is now fixed since these shutters were destroyed by a fire in 1988. On the left the imposing main meeting room remains intact with a panelled dado and fixed seats on the side walls, raised over the stand, which is up three steps with a panelled front and two flights of stairs for access. The shutters can still be raised into the roof and contain a double door allowing access when the shutters are down (Fig 4.25a). Similar designs with double shutters also survive at Pickering (1793) (Fig 4.25b) and Malton (1823), both in North Yorkshire.

Two West Country meeting houses less than ten miles apart demonstrate some of the further diversity in 19th-century meeting

Fig 4.25
The double-shuttered meeting house design (a) on the left the remaining full-height shutter at Uxbridge contains a double door to the men's meeting room; (b) at Pickering both sets of shutters remain in the central corridor although, at half-height, only allowing limited vision between the two meeting rooms.

houses. About a mile and a half from the Devon village of Uffculme, the original Spiceland Meeting House was rebuilt in 1815 by a local builder, Daniel Henson, in a manner which has more of the 18th century in it (Fig 4.26). The four-bay frontage of a rectangular plan has an arched doorway in the second bay with three round-headed windows, the two on the left lighting the main meeting room and that on the right the smaller women's room. The walls are of local rubblestone and are capped with a hipped slate roof. Inside, the pine ministers' stand is on two levels, rather similar to that at Farfield, except that the lower benches return a little way along the side walls: it is fronted by panelling surmounted with a rail. In front of it hangs a timber and iron chandelier (Fig 4.27). To the rear of the room is a gallery which is stepped forward at either end, one of these concealing the inner porch. The wall beneath the gallery is partly panelled with what were originally moveable shutters.

In contrast, the 1845 meeting house at Wellington in Somerset could from the outside be the type specimen for the gable-end entrance meeting house built for any one of a range of Nonconformist denominations. It was designed by a Quaker railway engineer, Francis Fox, a member of one of the dominant families in the town, and is on a relatively small site behind the houses on the High Street. The plan appears very nearly square and presents the gable end towards the street with a central door with a pedimented wooden canopy over (Fig 4.28). This is flanked by two small 12-paned sash windows with three similar above, all with segmentally curved arches. The walls are of brick on a stone plinth and rise at the front to a simple stone cornice and a pedimented gable, pierced by a circular window or oculus. The side walls are blind and the only other windows are in the rear gable end, which contains two 20-paned sash windows lighting the main meeting room.

The interior is, however, definitively Quaker. The door gives onto a lobby with access to the two side-by-side meeting rooms, the men's on the left and the smaller women's meeting room on the right. Stairs rise to a stepped L-shaped gallery which covers both the lobby and the women's meeting room. This has a panelled front which still retains its original gas-light fittings. The screen between the two rooms is decorated with pilasters and still has functioning shutters: the ministers' stand opposite is on two levels as at Uffculme and has a panelled front. The design is most ingenious in its use of the very limited space, both to provide two interlinked meeting houses and maximise the amount of seating (Fig 4.29).

Other denominations at this period were increasingly designing meeting houses in the Gothic style, of which Wellington shows no sign. However, later in the century, even Quakers were not immune to the attractions of Gothic. At Scholes, near Cleckheaton in West Yorkshire, in 1883 William Henry Thorp designed a perfect small Gothic meeting house for the reintroduction of Quaker worship in the area, supported by the

Fig 4.26
Spiceland meeting house at Uffculme in Devon, built in 1815, but with a decidedly more 18th-century appearance.

Fig 4.27
The meeting room at Spiceland with its timber and iron chandelier and the narrow style of ministers' stand with seats at a lower level at the side, very similar to that at Farfield.

Fig 4.28
The chapel-like exterior of Wellington meeting house of 1845, with its gable-end entrance topped with an impressive wooden canopy.

Fig 4.29
The interior of the main meeting room at Wellington taken from the gallery, which in this case is on two sides of the room. The ministers' stand on the left faces the shutters which can open to reveal the women's meeting room, which has part of the gallery above it.

Crosland family. It is built of coursed rubble and ashlar dressings with buttresses, and arched windows with leaded lights, lancet-like in the gable ends, and even a stone fleur de lys finial on the gable apex. The meeting house has a red-tiled roof and sits in a wonderfully orderly graveyard with completely uniform headstones (Fig 4.30). The inside has exposed brick walls with panelling to dado level and is open to the roof trusses. The most strikingly Gothic internal detail is the ministers' stand, which has a wooden curved sounding board above, which evokes the canon's stalls in a modest medieval cathedral (Fig 4.31). To the rear is a porch leading to a lobby which has been reconfigured more than once to give modern facilities, although the basement, which held the original heating boiler, is still accessible.

Two years earlier, Friends at Frandley in Cheshire rebuilt their 17th-century meeting house in a pared-down Gothic style. Here the material is red brick with sandstone and terracotta detailing, the bays in the side walls are separated by buttresses, and all the windows are tall and narrow with semi-circular heads. The entrance in the front gable end was originally protected by a porch: both the gables have three stepped tall windows (Fig 4.32). The entrance gives onto a full-width lobby with a staircase leading up to the stepped gallery above. The lobby is separated from the meeting room by a fixed pine partition. The meeting room is, like Scholes, open to the roof trusses. The partition is panelled, as is the front of the gallery, and the panels are filled with diagonal boarding; the walls of both lobby and meeting room have a wooden dado which rises over the stand which fills the wall at the far end. The whole has a restrained yet elegant feel.

To one side of the meeting is a building, referred to as the Sunday school, although built in 1726 as a stable with schoolroom over, as at Brigflatts. It has an external staircase to allow access to the upper floor, which acts as a porch to the entrance to the lower floor. The current name reminds us that Sunday, or more properly, First-day, schools were a feature of Quaker meetings, just as in all other churches at this period.

Another gable-end meeting house, although with a Classical front

Fig 4.30
Scholes meeting house within its burial ground.

Fig 4.31
The ministers' stand at Scholes.

elevation, is that in Hastings. This is an example of a meeting house built not for resident Friends but for summer visitors to a resort. Affluent Victorian Quakers were inclined to take a house in a resort town for the summer. Indeed, Henry Pease of Darlington was instrumental in the 1860s in developing the resort of Saltburn-on-Sea, conveniently situated and connected by rail with the family businesses in Middlesbrough and Darlington. Summer resort meeting houses were built, often funded by wealthy Friends, in more than 15 resorts and still survive, though now hosting a regular meeting for worship, in Ilkley (1869), Jersey (1872) and Colwyn Bay (1890).

The story at Hastings is that after an abortive start in the 1830s, Friends were meeting by 1859 in a reading room on the front. The

Fig 4.32
Frandley meeting house. The extent of the former porch can be clearly seen on the gable end wall.

Monthly Meeting were cautious about the need for a meeting house, but in 1864 they agreed to investigate the possibility because Friends who holidayed in Hastings were 'prepared to exert themselves in order to obtain funds for the erection of a Meeting House'. The instigator was Edwin Ransome of Ipswich, and within the month he had purchased a site, commissioned the Quaker architect William Beck to design a meeting house, and got together a committee to oversee the project. Beck's original design was for a single-storey building, but after accommodation for a caretaker was added, a change to a two-storey elevation became essential.[4]

The meeting house is sandwiched between two sizeable villas and is on a T-shaped plan with the bar of the T towards the street. This contained cloakrooms, the caretaker's accommodation and a lobby which led into the meeting room. This was built of yellow brick with a pitched slate roof topped with ventilators; each side wall contains three sets of windows, each consisting of two arched windows with a small circular window in the apex, separated by shallow brick buttresses. The street elevation is stuccoed, painted and of three bays, the central one containing the pedimented entrance with a decorated cornice and above it a quatrefoil window. The flanking bays were intended to have windows similar to those in the side walls, but are now plain oblongs set in arched openings. Four wall strips edge the bays and, above the entablature, become short pilasters breaking up the parapet which hides the roof from the street (Fig 4.33).

Fig 4.33
Hastings meeting house.

The meeting room itself is a well-proportioned and well-lit space with a suspended ceiling, below which show two tie-beams with braces supported on plain corbels. There is a dado rail at sill level. The meeting room was designed and, after some misgivings, built, remarkably, with no ministers' stand. This is perhaps the earliest example of what was, towards the end of the century, as we shall see, to become the rule.

As a result of government action in the 1850s, burial grounds in cities and large towns were closed for health reasons. Quakers were one group which had to decide whether to find new burial grounds or to use the new municipal cemeteries. As we have seen, in London the solution was to transfer burials to the grounds associated with suburban meetings like Brentford and Winchmore Hill. In Norwich, the burial ground associated with the Gildencroft meeting house was sufficiently far from the city to continue in use. Quakers in Bradford bought space in the private cemetery at Undercliffe and reinterred the bodies from their city-centre site. Friends in Manchester and Leeds opened new burial grounds at Ashton-on-Mersey and Adel, respectively. In both these cases, meeting houses were built for the use solely of meetings associated with burials and included a cottage for a resident caretaker. Both burial grounds contain lettered stones which mark out the grid on which the burials were placed, as seen at Winchmore Hill.

At Ashton-on-Mersey (1856) the architect was Peter Alley, the partner of Richard Lane, who had designed the Mount Street meeting house. He designed a two-storey brick structure with the meeting room on the upper floor, the ground floor being used for stables and a coach house. In the early 20th century the stables were enclosed for use as a meeting room, regular worship having started as soon as 1860 (now known as Sale Meeting) (Fig 4.34a). At Adel (1872) the buildings were designed by a local architect, Edward Birchall, who had already designed the new meeting house of 1868 in the city at Carlton Hill. The Adel meeting house is a more modest single-storey chapel-like brick structure with a slate roof, the original entrance in the gable end (Fig 4.34b). A regular meeting was not established here until 1923; since 2007 the premises have been entered from an extension at the rear of the meeting house which neatly echoes the original design.

Fig 4.34
Meeting houses at burial grounds (a) Sale meeting house, Ashton-on-Mersey (on the left). The arched openings on the lower floor were originally open to the elements and were used as stables and carriage sheds; (b) Adel meeting house behind the caretaker's cottage at the entrance to the burial ground.

Mission work and adult schools

Adult schools did not originate with Friends, but they were early in adopting them as a form of outreach to the working class. Joseph Sturge (1793–1859), a Birmingham Friend and one of the leaders of the British and Foreign Anti-Slavery Society, opened an adult school in Birmingham in 1845, originally on Sunday evenings but soon moved to Sunday mornings. The initial focus was on reading and writing for young working men, often using the Bible as a text, but soon broadened to include men of all ages and then women. A national body, the Friends First Day School Association was formed in 1847 and the work gradually spread through the country in the 1860s and 1870s, expanding to include lectures on a variety of subjects, recreational activities, savings funds and libraries: by 1900 there were thought to be 25,000 scholars involved. Originally using school premises and ancillary rooms in meeting houses, it was not long before meeting house premises became adapted to accommodate the adult school and additional facilities built into new meeting houses or added to old ones.

At Stafford, for instance, in 1892 a room was built onto the back of the neat 1730 meeting house with toilets and a kitchen for adult school work – this is still known as the Institute. However, by 1906 there was a need for more space, and a large corrugated iron mission hall was erected on the burial ground at the front, completely obscuring the original building from the road.

Adult school work was also capable of resurrecting dormant meetings, as for instance at Beccles, where no meetings had been held since 1816. The institution of schools for men and women led to expansion of the buildings in 1909, an extra storey being added to the meeting house and a school room to the rear.

At Croydon, there was also considerable adult school activity, which led first to the building of a block of classrooms in 1883 between the 1816 meeting house and the burial ground (given by John Horniman) and then

Fig 4.35
The interior of the Adult School Hall at Croydon, showing the exposed roof trusses which evoke a medieval aisled barn, perfectly lit by windows at ground floor and clerestory.

in 1908 to the building of an Adult School Hall (funded by G Theodore Crosfield). This is the only part of the complex to survive a 1940 bombing raid, but it remains as a tribute to the ambition and success of this exercise in outreach which boasted 1,000 members in 1908. The hall is a remarkable structure in an Arts & Crafts idiom by the architect William Curtis Green. The outside presents a large barn-like structure with low brick walls surmounted by a deep pantile roof and clerestory windows. The inside resembles nothing as much as a medieval aisled tithe barn and has a remarkable timber roof structure comprising a set of scissor trusses. The main lighting comes from the clerestory, but both gable ends also contain a tall five-part window; at one end there is a platform (Fig 4.35). The architect exhibited the design that year at the Royal Academy and included it with his nomination papers for the RIBA the following year.

However, this impressive building is completely outclassed by the Institute buildings designed for adult school work in Moseley Road, Birmingham, by the brothers Ewan and James Harper. They were commissioned by Richard Cadbury[5] to bring together ongoing work at three sites and completed in 1897, and were built of red brick with terracotta dressings. They comprised a front block with coffee room, library and lecture hall, a central block of 37 classrooms on two floors, and at the rear the Large Hall, capable of seating 2,000, built over a basement used as a gymnasium. This meeting hall had a platform at one end, above which an organ was installed; a horseshoe-shaped gallery on three sides supported by reeded columns which ascended above the gallery parapet to support the arcade above; the whole surmounted by a clerestory. The end opposite the platform contained two three-light windows with arched tops stretching from floor to ceiling. The ceiling itself was panelled, with beams and pendant bosses (Fig 4.36).

The hall was intended solely for adult school work and not for worship, although the Yearly Meeting gathered there when it met in Birmingham in 1954. It is now occupied by a Pentecostal church.

Fig 4.36
The Large Hall of the Birmingham Institute, designed for Richard Cadbury by the Harper brothers, 1897, now adapted for use by a Pentecostal church.

Fig 4.37
The Mission Hall of 1903 (on the right) dwarfs the original meeting house (on the left) at East Harling, Norfolk. Both are now in residential use.

Fig 4.38 (below left)
Pakefield meeting house of 1833: a modest building within a walled burial ground.

Fig 4.39 (below right)
Pakefield mission hall of 1898, every inch a dissenters' gable-end chapel, complete with four named foundation stones under the windows.

Although adult schools were usually held on a Sunday, scholars were not encouraged to join the local meeting for worship; rather, special worship services were provided in what Quakers no doubt felt was a more approachable style, with Sankey and Moody[6] choruses and a short prepared 'message'. Such mission meetings became widespread, and a Friends Home Mission Committee was set up by Yearly Meeting in 1882 to coordinate the work, and in some places 'missioners' were appointed to carry it out.

This was the case in East Harling, Norfolk, where a mission hall of nearly twice its size was built adjacent to the small simple meeting house in 1903, in red brick with terracotta dressings, containing a large platform at one end and seats for 200 (Fig 4.37). The last remaining mission hall in active use is at Pakefield, just to the south of Lowestoft. Here there is a meeting house and burial ground (Fig 4.38); further from the sea, in St Georges Road, is the mission hall completed in 1898, like East Harling very chapel-like in its appearance, and complete with inscribed

Fig 4.40
The interior of the Pakefield mission hall, complete with heating stove (left foreground) and the railed dais at the far end.

foundation stones (Fig 4.39). It is in red brick with contrasting brick details and a slate roof. The entrance in the gable end is protected by a small porch with three stone plaques above set in a triangle and inscribed in relief 'FRIENDS MISSION HALL'. On one side are four casement windows, whereas the other side, facing the neighbouring house, is blind with rooflights. Internally, the single room has a wooden dado, a heating stove with a metal back leading to the external chimney, and a dais at one end surrounded by a timber rail with turned balusters (Fig 4.40).

Quakerism transformed

The evangelical thrust of mid-19th-century Quakerism was challenged in the 1890s by younger members of the Society who wished to incorporate the developments in biblical studies, history and in science into their world view and to combat the anti-intellectualism they saw in traditional Quakerism. At a conference called by the Home Mission Committee in Manchester in 1895 to educate younger Friends and to strengthen ministry, these more liberal Friends became a visible presence. The movement led to a series of summer schools, in which Friends concentrated on the results of scholarly study of Quakerism and English society, and eventually to the founding in 1903 of Woodbrooke in Birmingham as a Quaker college.

These liberals went back to the founding Quaker experience of God as the 'Light Within' or the 'Inward Teacher' and saw George Fox as a mystic, part of the long religious tradition which William James highlighted in his Gifford Lectures of 1901/2.[7] Although evangelical language and modes of worship did not disappear from British Quakerism until the middle of the 20th century, the Society had once again undergone a major transformation.

At the same time, the influence of the recorded ministers, who had dominated worship in the previous two centuries, was waning, and this is seen architecturally in the decline of the ministers' stand. As we

Fig 4.41
Birkenhead meeting house showing the windows of the meeting room with the caretaker's accommodation at the left.

Fig 4.42
Edgbaston meeting house, simple yet elegant in its Classical detailing.

have observed, it was possible for a resort meeting house in the 1860s to be built without a stand, but during the 1870s and 1880s it was still rare for a new meeting house to be built without one. Things changed completely from the 1890s onwards and it became rare for a stand to be built. Meeting houses were either built with the balustraded dais seen in mission halls, or with an open platform or with no focus for the worship at all. Yearly Meeting in 1904 acknowledged these changes in recommending 'that in the building of new meeting houses … the [stand] should be made less conspicuous; and that all seats should be so placed as to make it easy for Friends to speak from any part of the meeting house'.[8]

Two meeting houses of the 1890s which show the transition are at Birkenhead, Merseyside, and Edgbaston, Birmingham. At Birkenhead in 1892, Friends built their second meeting house in 50 years to a design by George Grayson, best known for his public buildings at Port Sunlight. It is built of red brick with stone dressings and consists of three parts: towards the road is a two-storey structure, vaguely domestic in appearance with a projecting gabled bay, which contains a lobby and cloakrooms with classrooms above; this leads to a meeting room of four bays with mullioned and transomed windows with leaded glazing separated by brick buttresses; behind this is an attached cottage for a caretaker (Fig 4.41). Unusually for Friends, the windows in the meeting house have a border of plain red stained glass. The meeting room has a pine dado which rises over the built-in bench on a platform, which is all that remains of a ministers' stand, whose original balustrade has now been removed.

Edgbaston was built in 1893 for a new suburban meeting formed 20 years before. The architect was William Henman and the L-shaped plan had two unlinked meeting rooms at right angles with a single-storey range to the side containing cloakrooms and toilets. The main entrance is on the corner of this ancillary range and is of stone with a pedimented stone portico and pilasters surrounding a semi-circular arched doorway. The building is of red brick and its Classical detailing includes gable ends with broken pediments and a number of Venetian windows lighting the meeting rooms (Fig 4.42). The main meeting room has a vertically boarded dado to sill height and at the far end a narrow platform with an iron balustrade and no fixed seating, its importance marked by a central pediment with entablature and pilasters on the wall behind.

Far to the north, in Dundee, a completely different sort of building was designed in 1893 for a small group of Friends meeting at that time in the YMCA. The architects were Malcolm Stark and Fred Rowntree, then practising together in Glasgow: Fred was a Quaker from the Scarborough branch of the family which also produced the chocolate manufacturers of York. The Dundee site had been gifted by a wealthy Friend and was on one of the fashionable streets in the city centre. The original request was for a single-storey building but, to satisfy the formula for development being enforced by the city engineer, a five-storey structure with a shop front was erected (Fig 4.43). The meeting room was originally on the ground floor and had a cast iron gallery. Much of the property was let to various tenants.

A major influence on meeting house architecture at this time was the Arts & Crafts movement. It is seen clearly in the meeting house at Bournville built in 1905 in the centre of the village which Richard and George Cadbury had laid out for their workers when they moved chocolate production out of the centre of Birmingham from 1879. The design of the meeting house was by William Alexander Harvey who was architect for the Bournville Village Trust (1895–1904). The meeting room is a large barn-like space four bays deep, with a wagon roof with the trusses rising from the floor, and lit at ground level by three- or four-light segmentally arched windows and in the roof by a series of dormer windows (Fig 4.44). It could well be a precursor of the Croydon Adult School Hall.

The hall has a vertically boarded dado and at one end a platform on three steps with a large arched panel above surmounted with a biblical text. In the original design the platform was a dais with a surrounding balustrade and steps at the side (Fig 4.45). Over the entrance lobby is a gallery which contains the organ installed in 1915 – unique for a British meeting house.

However, it is the frontage which is the most remarkable feature. Above the central semi-circular arched doorway with its multiply stepped

Fig 4.43
Dundee meeting house, designed in 1893 to fit in with the other buildings on this fashionable street. When the picture was taken, the ground floor was let to an estate agency.

Fig 4.44
Bournville meeting house
showing the interior with roof
trusses reaching to the floor
and the rear gallery with, on
either side, the organ pipes.

Fig 4.45
The design of the platform as
a railed dais at the time of the
opening of Bournville meeting
house in 1907.

Fig 4.46
Bournville: wrought iron
supports for the rainwater
goods in Arts & Crafts style.

Fig 4.47
*Bournville meeting house,
the front elevation with the
front elevation of the First
Church of Christ Scientist,
Manchester by Edgar Wood
(inset) for comparison.*

brick head is a tall two-light window with stone mullions and transoms, and above that in the gable apex a sundial with the inscription 'MY. TIMES.ARE.IN.THY.HAND'. To the left and right are short single-storey wings splayed in a Y shape and in the angle of the left bay and the gable an octagonal turret containing the stair to the gallery at the rear of the meeting room. The rainwater goods in the wings and on the turret are supported by extravagantly long curved wrought iron brackets (Fig 4.46). This frontage bears so many similarities to Edgar Wood's design for the First Church of Christ Scientist, Manchester (1903), that it is hard to believe that it is not a deliberate homage (Fig 4.47).

A more clearly Arts & Crafts design is that by the Quaker architect Fred Rowntree for the Hampstead meeting house, built in 1907 for a meeting founded in 1898. On a small and awkwardly shaped plot on the corner of Heath Street and Hampstead Square, a building of three floors, including basement, was built. The gabled Heath Street frontage is stuccoed and has the entrance up three steps under a timber porch supported by Doric columns and a semi-domed roof covered in copper, with a two-light casement to the right and above a four-light, vaguely Venetian, window. The elevation on Hampstead Square has the lower part of the wall as bare red brick with stucco above; towards the front, the upper floor is lit by a four-light dormer window, then comes a chimney stack with small brick buttress, and finally the gabled end of the meeting room with three square casements in curved recesses with external shutters and a circular oculus in the gable apex (Fig 4.48).

Inside, the decor is plain with some Arts & Crafts detailing. A lobby

Fig 4.48
Hampstead meeting house, side elevation on Hampstead Square, as shown in the architect's drawing used for the invitation card for the official opening in 1907. [With thanks to Roger Button]

Fig 4.49
Golders Green meeting house, a gentle evocation of a 17th-century meeting house.

with staircase leading up to the library and down to the basement gives onto a small committee room and, straight ahead, the meeting room, which has a wooden dado with windows above in arched recesses. After some difficulty, apparently, it was decided to have no stand or platform.[9]

Fred Rowntree also designed Golders Green Meeting House in 1913. This is on one corner of North Square in Hampstead Garden Suburb, but makes no attempt to compete with Lutyens' grand church buildings for the Anglicans and Free Churches. A modest building of brick and tile, it was inspired by the meeting house at Jordans, but without attempting any kind of copy (Fig 4.49).

This is in direct contrast to the building which became the meeting house in the first garden city at Letchworth. Howgills was a house designed for Juliet Reckitt in 1907, which contained a hall intended for religious purposes and was given to the Society in that same year, with

Fig 4.50
Howgills, Letchworth meeting house, showing the double-gabled entrance front in fine Arts & Crafts style with, on the right, the reproduction of the front elevation of Brigflatts meeting house, complete with two-storey porch.

Fig 4.51
The meeting room at Howgills, as near a copy of Brigflatts as modernity would allow.

the rest of the house. Its former owner retained a flat, gifted in 1909. The architects were Robert Bennett and Benjamin Bidwell, the latter a Quaker, former associates of Barry Parker and Raymond Unwin, the chief architects of the garden city.

Howgills is built on an L-shaped plan with two frontages; the entrance to the house has twin gables and a central chimney and presents an Arts & Crafts face to the world, with a deep-set arched doorway and the mullioned windows of a typical north-country house of the 17th century. At right angles to this, the other frontage reproduces that of Brigflatts, with a two-storey porch and pairs of mullioned windows at either end. The two full-height windows to the right of the porch are here much larger nine-paned mullioned and transomed windows to give extra light to the meeting room which lies behind (Fig 4.50). This too is modelled on Brigflatts, with a staircase leading from the porch to serve the balustraded galleries on two sides of the room: these are supported on turned timber posts which continue as plain rectangular posts to meet the beamed ceiling (Fig 4.51). There are two major indications that we are in the early 20th century and not the 17th – the complete absence of a ministers' stand or even a platform and the presence in the gable wall of a large fireplace with carved overmantel, said to be early work of Eric Gill.

Just as the Arts & Crafts movement was trying to recapture the old values of the imagined artist-craftsman of the past and reassert them in an age of mass production, so there was a thread in turn-of-the-century Quakerism which was attempting to recapture the immediacy of the spiritual life of the early Friends from the accretions and formulas of evangelical religion. Returning to the past by revisiting the places in Cumbria where the early Society had been formed – '1652 country' – and building meeting houses in the style of those early Friends were ways to effect that transformation, but not ultimately successful ones. It needed spiritual challenges to reawaken the Society of Friends and the 20th century was to provide plenty of those.

Notes

1   Watts 1995, 332.
2   This was William Lucas of Hitchin (1804–61) in 1834, as quoted in Butler 1999a, 658.
3   *The British Friend* was one of two Quaker periodicals, both starting publication in 1843, the other being *The Friend,* which took opposite sides in the conservative/evangelical divide. *The British Friend* ceased publication in 1913: *The Friend* continues to this day.
4   The story of the building of Hastings meeting house is well told in Radice 2016.
5   Richard Cadbury (1835–99) and his brother George (1839–1922) took over the family chocolate business in 1861, and in 1879 moved it to open country south of Birmingham city centre in what was to become the model village of Bournville.
6   Dwight Moody and Ira Sankey were American evangelists who visited Britain in 1873 and who were responsible for introducing gospel songs into evangelical meetings. Their hymnbook *Sacred Songs and Solos* (1873) was influential among Nonconformists for generations.
7   James 1902.
8   Quoted in Butler 1999a, 897.
9   *The Friend* 1902, 789, as quoted in Butler 1999a, 402.

5 Into the modern age and beyond

Quaker buildings 1915–2020

T he beginning of the 20th century saw Quakers, along with other dissenters, at the heart of government. The northern and Midland industrial cities, where dissenters and the Liberal party, which they largely supported, had their power base, had come to be very influential on the national scene. The abolition of compulsory church rates[1] in 1868 had removed the last hurdle to Quakers becoming ordinary citizens. The same year had seen John Bright, a Quaker from Rochdale, become a member of Gladstone's cabinet as President of the Board of Trade, and Friends had been active in Liberal administrations from that point. Quakers, particularly from those wealthy families who had thrived in business and banking, were attending the universities and gradually invading the professions from which they had earlier been excluded: in 1890 they set up a national school at Reading – Leighton Park, the 'Quaker Eton' – to educate young Quakers to the standard required for university entrance.

However, the ending of the Quaker distinctives, and full engagement with the world made for difficulties over a united Quaker witness to the world. That world was rigidly class-based and Quakers were part of it, largely, as we have seen, of the middle classes. Although Friends had been active proponents of the 'social gospel' going back at least to the pioneering prison-visiting work of Elizabeth Fry (born Gurney) in the 1820s, on the whole they did not wish to disrupt the social order. The witness to equality was not seen as a call to socialist revolution, rather as a gentler assertion of spiritual equality. As we have seen, the education of the poor in adult schools was not intended to make them into Quakers, but rather worshippers in Friends Mission Halls.

Greater disagreements were to arise over the Quaker opposition to war as a way of settling international disputes (the peace testimony). Friends were split in their attitudes to the Boer War (1899–1902) when a few eminent Friends publicly supported the war despite the fervent opposition of the younger liberal and more socially committed Quakers. Worse was to come in 1914 when not only did the leading Quaker member of Asquith's cabinet, Jack Pease, not resign with others when war was declared, but some prominent Friends were soon calling for young Quaker men to enlist. Nevertheless, the Yearly Meeting maintained a firm opposition to the war and, when it came in 1916, to conscription, supporting the newly acquired right to conscientious objection, which Quaker MPs had done much to introduce, even for men not members of the Society. In the end, only two-thirds of young adult Quakers became conscientious objectors and there continued to be disagreements among Friends both over military action itself and about the degree to which the alternative service which was offered acted to support the war by freeing others to fight. These arguments caused dissension within the Friends Ambulance Unit, set up by some Quakers to provide alternative service, but never an official Quaker body.

In contrast, the Friends War Victims Relief Committee, originally formed to relieve suffering for non-combatants in the Franco-Prussian War in 1870, was an official Quaker group and was formally reconstituted in 1914 to provide relief initially to Belgian refugees and then in devasted areas of France, Serbia and Russia, latterly in association with the equivalent body of American Quakers. In the 1939–45 war this collaboration was again active, first on the home front and then in mainland Europe, leading to the award of the Nobel Peace Prize to British and American Quakers in 1947.

If relief of the victims of war was the main thrust of Quaker peace work in the first half of the 20th century, the second half of the century saw the switch to a more political focus in opposition to the use of nuclear weapons. The establishment of the United Nations led to Quaker organisations in Geneva and New York which lobbied successfully for international action in the areas of peace and peacekeeping, such as child soldiers and non-combatants in civil wars. Towards the end of the century the main focus for Quaker work became environmental and social, with the awareness of climate change leading to a call from the Yearly Meeting of 2011 for British Friends to become a low-carbon sustainable community.

Quaker discipline, which had acted as a protective hedge around the Society since the early 18th century and had been enshrined in the extracts from Yearly Meeting minutes kept in the Books of Discipline, had been relaxed during the latter half of the 19th century and now sat more lightly with Friends. Elders and overseers were still active in monitoring gently the behaviour of other Quakers, but disownment became a thing of the past. The advent of a liberal theology also diminished the importance of orthodoxy and the decreasing importance of recorded ministers, which we have seen already reflected in the disappearance of the ministers' stand, was confirmed by the cessation of recording in 1924. The Book of Discipline changed through the 20th century to become an anthology of current Quaker thought, renewed about every generation, to which were attached those regulations needed to keep the organisation running.

As the Society became more open, its numbers began to grow again, gaining members from those in the wider society attracted by Quaker principles and flexible approach to Christianity, largely from the peace movement and what came to be known as the caring professions. This move from a Society in which members had been largely brought up as Quakers to one in which the majority, as in the 17th century, were 'Quakers by convincement' had a major effect. Those who attended Quaker meetings but who did not become members – known as 'attenders' – also grew in numbers across the century. Numbers of members peaked in around 1960 at 21,000, but total numbers including attenders stood at around 30,000 for most of the last half of the century before starting to decline around 2000.

The building of Friends House

Whereas in previous centuries Quaker action in the world, as for instance the movement for the abolition of slavery, were the concern of individual Quakers and informal groups of Friends, the later 19th and early 20th centuries saw an increased centralisation of this work, first under committees of the Yearly Meeting (for example the Home Mission Committee, *see* page 90) and then gradually by paid staff. The growth of central structures brought with it the need for suitable accommodation.

The Yearly Meeting had had its work centred for many years in a maze of buildings at Devonshire House on the edge of the City, in a block bordered by Houndsditch and Bishopsgate. It comprised 5 committee rooms, 21 other rooms used as offices, 4 strong rooms, the library and the Institute. By the 1910s there were nearly 50 staff members working in dimly lit offices amidst a rabbit warren of corridors and staircases, conditions which could be fairly described as Dickensian. At the same time, the two Yearly Meeting Houses built in 1793/4 on the same site, one of which was now redundant following the merger of the men's and women's Yearly Meetings in 1896, occupied much space but were used rarely.

In 1911 the decision was made that this situation could not continue and a Special Premises Committee was set up to consider the options, whether it be refurbishment or rebuilding on the current or a new site. The possibilities of not having the offices and the Yearly Meeting House on the same site, or even of hiring an existing public hall for the Yearly Meeting were to be entertained. Quakers as a body and all the committees charged with overseeing the decision were divided on these matters, and the stage was set for what became a 16-year saga including the hiatus caused by the 1914–18 war.

Eventually it was decided to relocate to the Bloomsbury area. After considering the site where Senate House was later to be built, and after long but eventually fruitless negotiations to buy the buildings which Lutyens had built for the Theosophical Society in Tavistock Square,[2] it was decided to buy the site on the Euston Road then occupied by Endsleigh Gardens[3] when it came up for sale in 1923.

A competition was held for the design, adjudicated by W Curtis Green, architect of the Croydon Adult School Hall, and four Quaker architects were invited to submit. The specification included a large meeting house to hold 1,500 people and a smaller for 200–300, offices for letting to provide regular income to help maintain the building, and the replacement of the offices, library, strong rooms and Institute that had been available at Devonshire House, the whole occupying the western half of the site. The only aesthetic requirement was that the building should be 'simple and dignified'. The eastern portion of the site facing St Pancras Church was to be sold for other building and to raise funds for the construction, with a portion retained to provide a garden to make up in some degree for the loss of amenity caused by building on an open space.

The winning design was provided by Hubert Lidbetter (1885–1966), a Dublin-born Quaker whose career had been disrupted by the war and who had recently begun to practise in London. His design divided the building into three equal blocks, each with its own entrance, which

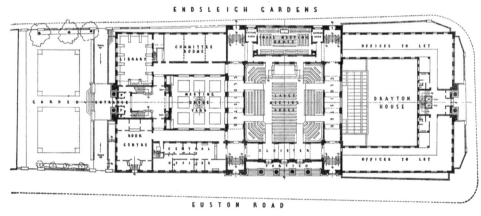

Fig 5.1
Friends House – the north elevation on Euston Road as built 1925.

Fig 5.2
Friends House – plan as finally built 1925. [Drawing by Hubert Lidbetter]

could be linked if required. The central block contained the two meeting rooms and was entered from the Euston Road, the western one was for commercial letting and was entered from Gordon Place, and the eastern block contained the offices and committee rooms for the Society and was entered from the garden. Either side of the central block, the side blocks enclosed two courtyards (Figs 5.1 and 5.2).

Overall, the appearance was Classical, austere rather than simple, and intended to sit comfortably within its environment. Curtis Green, the assessor, described it as 'direct simple and straightforward' and 'pleasantly reminiscent of the eighteenth century'. Windows on the three main frontages were wooden sashes, matching the domestic buildings it then faced across Euston Square, and the entrance porticos were supported by Doric columns, which not only followed Quaker precedent (as at Norwich,

Fig 5.3
Friends House, details of the penultimate bay at the west end of the north elevation showing the decorative detail.

see Figure 4.6) but echoed the Doric arched entrance to Euston station. Now all this context has disappeared, the building appears both more monolithic and more grandiose than was intended.

The building is steel framed, covered in brick with Portland stone dressings, with each entrance being entirely faced with stone. There are three main storeys on a basement, with an additional attic storey: it was designed so that the addition of a mansard was possible. On the Euston Road each of the side blocks has ten bays, with the penultimate bay at either end marked with a balconied window in a stone architrave on the first floor and a round window with stone surround on the second. At the western end the ground floor of this bay was built to plan and has a large semi-circular window with stone surround; at the eastern end the door to the bookshop, added late in the day, replaced the ground-floor window (Fig 5.3). This north elevation is, however, dominated by the recessed portico with its four Doric columns with steps in between leading to the five double entrance doors to the meeting house foyer, the whole flanked on both sides by a bay framed by stone pilasters containing double

Fig 5.4
Friends House, the central portico in the north elevation, as built 1925.

fire-exit doors with a fanlight over and, on the first floor, a sash window (Fig 5.4). Above the portico is a cornice band which stretches the whole length of the building and separates off the attic storey.

This cornice band returns along the side elevations which each have ten bays of sash windows separated into two blocks of five. Between them is a recessed portico in stone containing a double entrance doorway with first-floor window above, flanked by two Doric columns and framed by stone pilasters (Fig 5.5). The rear elevation repeats the front to a large extent, except that the central section of seven bays projects with bays two and six recessed. The central three bays contain large semi-circular windows with metal frames which were designed to light the small meeting house (Fig 5.6).

Fig 5.5
Friends House, the east entrance portico.

Fig 5.6
Friends House, the central south elevation with its different fenestration.

This small meeting house was a wide but not very deep room of double height with a gallery on three sides, intended for the monthly meetings of the executive committee of the Society (the Meeting for Sufferings) (Fig 5.7). In the late 1980s it was divided in half by the insertion of a new floor and further committee rooms created underneath. The large meeting house occupied the majority of the central

Fig 5.7
Friends House, the interior of the small meeting house as built.

Fig 5.8
Friends House, the large meeting house as originally built, taken from the rear gallery, and showing the clerestory windows and side galleries.

block and had on three sides at ground-floor level a lobby and two wide side cloisters which looked out onto the courtyards. Above these Lidbetter designed three raked galleries with panelled fronts topped with cast iron railings, with the side galleries lit at the rear by metal-framed windows. The floor below was raked on three sides and was provided with cinema-style tip-up seats, as in a Methodist central hall: benches were provided in the galleries. The coffered ceiling, supported by square piers and pilasters was originally above a clerestory of oblong windows to give top light (Fig 5.8). For 30 years from the 1980s these were obscured by a suspended ceiling. It has often been suggested that the novel design for this large meeting house was inspired by the plan at Manchester Mount Street, which also had galleries over corridor space. Another possible model is offered by Frank Lloyd Wright's Unity Temple (1908) where light from the top and the gallery rear is combined with galleries constructed over corridors, which Wright refers to on plan as cloisters.

Construction began in late July 1924. The properties at Devonshire House were finally sold in 1925, with the site to be cleared by December, but the office accommodation at what was now known as 'Friends House' was not ready until early January, so a short hiatus ensued before occupation by the staff. The large meeting house was not ready until 1927, when Yearly Meeting was held there for the first time, and the western block, known as 'Drayton House' after George Fox's birthplace, followed in 1928. Hubert Lidbetter received the RIBA London Architectural Bronze Medal in 1926 for the best building erected in London that year and the *Architectural Review* described Friends House as 'eminently Quakerly' and said of the design that 'it unites common sense with just so much relief from absolute plainness as gives pleasure to the eye'.[4]

Meeting houses between the wars

Now that there was no longer any need for a ministers' stand within a meeting house and the demand was that ministry from any part of the room could be heard, as the brief for Friends House had insisted, it might have been expected that meeting house design would change. This was only slowly to happen and the major challenge for the meeting house architect in the mid-20th century was to provide, on as small a footprint as possible, sufficient spaces for the social and organisational success of a local meeting – classrooms, committee rooms, kitchens etc – without their functions disturbing the quiet necessary for a successful meeting for worship.

In the 1920s and 1930s the influence of Arts & Crafts design was still considerable and seems to have been the default style for meeting houses. The meeting house at Preston is a case in point. Friends sold their town-centre meeting house in 1925 and built their new meeting house on a more suburban site. It is on a T plan with the cross of the T containing a corridor leading from a lobby to the kitchen and separating the meeting room from classrooms. The meeting room itself is an open hall with an exposed arch-braced timber roof suggestive of Bournville, dado panelling and a small platform at one end. The exterior, vaguely Elizabethan but essentially modest, is in brick with a tiled roof. There is

Fig 5.9
*Preston meeting house, an
Arts & Crafts interpretation
of a traditional design. The
photovoltaic panels are a
21st-century addition.*

a gabled porch offset to one side with double entrance doors flanked by two modest windows. The meeting room, side on to the road, has three bays of mullioned and transomed windows separated by brick buttresses (Fig 5.9).

Subsequent additions have hidden most of the original external features of the meeting house at Welwyn Garden City by H C Lander (1926). The most striking feature remains, however: the square meeting room with its echoes of the Romanesque. The plaster ceiling is cross vaulted with the vaults brought down onto timber corner posts with arched openings, which contain on three sides three-light vertical oblong windows; there is a dado on the side walls with a continuous fixed bench beneath, harking back to earlier meeting house design (Fig 5.10).

Two meeting houses were built about the same time in the south of Birmingham. Both had their origins in the adult school and mission movements in the 1890s, but were looking for a new start. Selly Oak

Fig 5.10
*Welwyn Garden City meeting
house, the interior of the
meeting room showing one
quarter of the cross-vaulting
brought down onto timber
posts.*

Fig 5.11
*Selly Oak meeting house
(1926).*

Fig 5.12
*Northfield meeting house
(1930).*

meeting house (1926) was a gift from Edward Cadbury, the son of George
Cadbury, the co-founder of Bournville. It was designed by the Bournville
Village Trust architects, originally on a simple T plan with the entrance in
the crosspiece. The meeting room is of four bays with casement windows,
the bays separated externally by buttresses; there is a small platform
at one end. From the road the appearance of the end gable is quite
imposing, with the single-storey block in front more domestic in style: the
brick walls are rendered in white and the roof is of clay tiles (Fig 5.11).
Northfield (1930), further south along the Bristol Road, was designed by
Quaker Ernest Hickman in a neo-Georgian style: it is in brick with clay tile
roofs and is on an I plan. The central meeting room has three large sash
windows to one side and on the other, two sashes separated by French
doors (Fig 5.12).

The meeting house at Keighley was built in 1936 to replace an older
building demolished for road widening. It is modest in size and built in
what was the garden of a private house and which is still maintained

as such. The domestic-looking building is of coursed sandstone with ashlar dressings and is on a T plan with a single-storey entrance block in the crossbar and the two-storey main block (the meeting room over a basement) leading away from it where the ground slopes downwards. There was originally a folding wooden screen separating the main room into a meeting space and committee room/library, suggestive of earlier meeting house plans. This was retained when the ancillary spaces were reordered in the 1990s (Fig 5.13).

Another modestly sized meeting house was built in 1937/8 in Malvern and designed by J R Armstrong, one of the Bournville Village Trust architects. The building is in buff brick with a grey tile roof and has the main meeting room parallel to the road, with a gabled entrance block under a hipped roof coming forward at one end. The architrave above the double doors has 'FRIENDS HOUSE' in bronze lettering; the doors give onto a lobby with toilets either side, a common feature. The meeting room is of four bays, two casement windows towards the road and three facing to the rear, the bays separated by buttresses. In the end gable is a tripartite window, the central segment arched, with beneath it a platform with the dado panelling which extends round the walls raised above it; the meeting room is open to the roof trusses. The meeting room has a set of furniture from Bryn Mawr, a Quaker initiative to provide work for the unemployed in South Wales (Fig 5.14).

Bryn Mawr furniture also features at Harrow meeting house, an Arts & Crafts-inspired building designed by Hubert Lidbetter and built in 1935. It is constructed in red brick with a steep tiled barn-like roof with low eaves, the gable ends rendered above ground-floor level. Raised central bays with a hipped roof to front and back each contain a nine-light mullioned and transomed window, with each light divided further into nine panes which provide the light for the main meeting room. The entrance leads to a lobby with toilets and offices and a classroom above reached by a stairway opposite the door. On the left, the doors to the meeting room reveal a large well-lit space with boarded dado around

Fig 5.13
Keighley meeting house
(1936).

Fig 5.14
Malvern meeting house
(1937/38).

Fig 5.15
Harrow meeting house
(1935), Hubert Lidbetter in
Arts & Crafts mode.

the walls; the upper classroom has a shuttered casement window above the door which overlooks the meeting room, perhaps a reference to the similar feature at Nailsworth (Fig 5.15).

Lidbetter also provided a design for the new meeting house in central Birmingham at Bull Street (1933), similar internally to his successful design for Friends House. This was originally of two storeys in brick with an artificial stone plinth and dressings, but was completely dwarfed by the neighbouring department store which had bought part of the site and occasioned the rebuilding. The side facing Bull Street still gives a sense of the design, which has brick pilasters separating the five bays, sash windows to the first floor with casements below, while the rest has been obscured by an added third storey and later buildings on the site

(Fig 5.16). Inside, the main meeting room has galleries over the lower corridors and is lit from above by clerestory windows as at Friends House. There is a small platform at one end and raked flooring at the sides; the seating is on benches (Fig 5.17).

Not far away in Sutton Coldfield, Lidbetter provided a design for the new meeting house, opened in 1939, which was to prove influential in the second half of the century. Its main distinctive feature was that the meeting house, a rectangular building with a hipped roof, had its main entrance in the short wall, with that entrance flanked by two projecting flat-roofed pavilions containing ancillary rooms. The materials were brick and tile and the left-hand pavilion was extended into a long block alongside the main meeting room. The ground sloped away on the other side and this allowed for a further room under the meeting room (Fig 5.18).

The double entrance doors are in a concrete surround with 'SOCIETY OF FRIENDS' engraved above and give onto a lobby area leading forward into the rectangular meeting room. This has a timber-panelled dado surround which is raised slightly at the far end. There are three small windows in the far wall, clerestory-level windows above the classroom block to the left, and three large windows on the right side, providing the majority of the lighting.

These three examples show that Lidbetter, the most influential architect of meeting houses at this period, although he had strong views on the appropriateness of rectangular meeting rooms, was otherwise not inflexible in the styles he used for meeting house exteriors, although he certainly did reuse elements of previous designs.

The distinctive features which characterised the Quaker meeting house in previous centuries have more or less disappeared in meeting houses built in the first half of the 20th century. Most meeting rooms are rectangular in shape with the entrance in a short wall and therefore with a definite orientation, sometimes emphasised by the existence of a low platform at one end. This implies that worshippers in general sat facing the front, probably with the elders in a row in front of them, much as in other chapels. Large barn-like spaces open to the roof are frequent, which

Fig 5.16
Hubert Lidbetter in neo-Georgian mode – Bull Street meeting house, Birmingham (1933), now completely dwarfed by surrounding buildings and with added third storey.

Fig 5.17
Bull Street meeting house, the main meeting room as originally built, showing the similarities to Friends House with clerestory and galleries and much closer in scale to Lloyd Wright's Unity Temple, which may have been an inspiration.

Fig 5.18
Sutton Coldfield meeting
house (1939) by Hubert
Lidbetter in modernist mode,
with its two side pavilions
which proved so influential
for later architects.

cannot have encouraged audibility from all sections of the room, as asked for by Yearly Meeting in 1904. The use of dado panelling below plastered walls is certainly an inheritance from earlier meeting houses, but whether this is assertion of a tradition or a touch of nostalgia is impossible to determine.

Reuse and adaptation of other buildings

Quakers in the 20th century began to reuse and repurpose other building types as meeting houses in much greater numbers than hitherto. This was perhaps a subconscious return to 17th-century practice, but more obviously an attempt to look for cheaper options as building costs rose. Many of these adapted buildings are houses of various sizes and dates whose ground floor reception rooms can be readily knocked together into a modestly sized meeting room, leaving rooms in the upper storeys to serve as caretaker's flats, offices and classrooms.

One of the most notable of these is the former St Laurence's Rectory, now Winchester meeting house, a substantial five-bay, three-storey Georgian town house of the 1770s in the centre of the city, close to the cathedral (Fig 5.19). It was purchased by Friends in 1973, originally with the aim of providing short-term emergency accommodation for people in need, as well as worship space. This particular service ceased in the 1990s and the meeting now lets six single rooms to tenants as well as providing space on the ground and first floors for letting to community groups.

The meeting house in Salisbury is a more eccentric building with a complex history. It consists of a small two-storey building with a bowed front and jettied upper storey, which was built in the 1830s and once

Fig 5.19
A most elegant dwelling house adaptation – Winchester meeting house, the former St Laurence's Rectory.

stood alone (Fig 5.20). Joined to it now is a long single-storey range with a doorway and another bow window to the front and which extends to the rear, probably dating from the 1850s. The whole is rendered and painted and under slate roofs. At the far end of this and further back from the road is a modern brick addition which contains the meeting house, which opened in 2010.

A building dating from 1740 has been the meeting house in Disley, Cheshire, since 1933. This stone-built slate-roofed group of buildings was once the Ring O'Bells public house with attached cottage and was converted to a teetotal village meeting place in the mid-19th century, two of the upper rooms being combined to create the meeting room which is still used by Friends. The cottage is now used by the warden (Fig 5.21a).

Another former public house, the Rose and Crown in Godmanchester, has served as Huntingdon meeting house since 1968/9. The L-shaped

Fig 5.20
An intriguing mixture of styles – Salisbury meeting house.

Fig 5.21
Former public houses as meeting houses (a) Disley meeting house (on the left); (b) Huntington meeting house (on the right).

building comprises a block on the street frontage of 18th-century origin in brick with a tiled hipped mansard roof: this is let out as flats. Leading back from this is a 17th-century block with a brick base and rendered timber framing above, topped by a steep thatched roof, now covered with corrugated iron. To the rear the meeting room was built, a brick structure with a tiled roof which may contain parts of an earlier structure (Fig 5.21b).

The meeting house in Kings Lynn, Norfolk, is in a building which from the early 17th century until 1970 was the Hulk Inn. The frontage still has that appearance and the old door retains its original stained glass. The meeting room is at the back and has been extended into the courtyard at the rear of the property.

Shops have been successfully adapted for use as meeting houses in a number of places. One of the most distinctive is that at Stocksfield in the Tyne Valley west of Newcastle. This is a former Cooperative store built for this mining community in around 1910 which, after closure, had a life as an art gallery and bookshop. It was offered to Friends by the owners in 1992. It still has its original timber shop front with a frieze with 'QUAKER MEETING HOUSE' now displayed over the recessed corner entrance. There are two meeting rooms, a kitchen and WC (Fig 5.22a).

A long-established meeting at Sawley in central Lancashire made the decision in 2016 to abandon its 18th-century meeting house in the remote countryside near Pendle Hill and relocate to the neighbouring town of Clitheroe. They have adapted shop and office premises near the town centre to give disabled access to a meeting room, a library and ancillary facilities. More recently, a new meeting in Newark, Nottinghamshire, has created its Quaker Centre in former shop premises in the centre of the town, near the market square, placing a glass roof over a courtyard to provide social space and creating a meeting room from rooms on the first floor (Fig 5.22b).

A more straightforward approach had been taken at the beginning of the 20th century on the outskirts of York when Friends in Acomb purchased a disused Primitive Methodist chapel on the village green. This unpretentious structure had been built in the early 19th century to designs by Henry Mainwaring. It presents its gable end to the green, this aspect containing two large sash windows with a smaller in the gable, with the entrance via a lobby area at the side. The meeting room, with a panelled dado, is at the rear with the library and small meeting room on two floors at the front.

Fig 5.22
Shops as meeting houses at (a) Stocksfield, Northumberland and (b) Newark, Nottinghamshire.

The meeting house in Littlehampton has a long history as a place of worship, having hosted Baptists, the Salvation Army and the Brethren before being bought by Friends in 1965. However, it was built in the 1830s as a Penny School with schoolmaster's house attached and it is the schoolroom in the main block which is used as the meeting room (Fig 5.23). The whole building is L-shaped and is in flint with brick quoins and dressings; the slate roof has gables over the school entrance on the right and over the house on the left. The meeting room is lit from both sides by windows of a decidedly Gothic design with pointed arches and Y-tracery. It has dado panelling and a flat ceiling. All the ancillary rooms are in the schoolmaster's house.

The meeting house in central Edinburgh is an ecclesiastical building on Victoria Terrace in the Old Town. It was built for the Original Secession Church in 1865 and bought by Friends in 1987 from the Boys Brigade who had already remodelled it extensively inside. The shops at ground-floor level had been adapted into a lobby and the church on the first floor had been divided vertically. Friends installed a lift and their meeting room is on the second floor. The exterior is in Italian Gothic style and is of four

Fig 5.23
Littlehampton meeting house,
a former Penny School.

bays and three storeys, the lower storey being fronted with an elegant arched loggia over the walkway of Victoria Terrace. The whole, although certainly not plain, fits well into the townscape as was initially intended.

Post-war meeting houses

The two decades that followed the war of 1939–45 saw the largest number of new meeting houses built in a similar period – 42 – nearly half the number built in the whole century. This was in part due to bomb damage to older meeting houses but also because of the replanning of town centres and their associated road networks which took place over the same period and which led both to compulsory purchase but also to meetings deciding to realise the increased value of their town centre sites and move to the suburbs.

In the London area the architect most used was Hubert Lidbetter, alone or together with his son Martin, who joined him in practice in 1950. The Lidbetters held successively the post of surveyor to Six Weeks Meeting[5] in which the ownership of all meeting houses within the greater London area was vested, and this meant they were well known to prospective clients. Meetings tended to employ local as well as Quaker architects, of whom the most notable at this time were perhaps Paul Mauger (1896–1962) and Norman Frith (1914–2015).

The architecture of this period has not received uniformly good opinions from later commentators, but the best of it shows a willingness to embrace new materials and to rethink old solutions. In particular, we see the beginnings of a new approach to the design of meeting rooms to take account of the move to worshipping in a circle of chairs centred on a table, which became the dominant layout.

For Quakers in Essex, the Lidbetter partnership designed in 1957 a modest domestic meeting house for Brentwood, a meeting founded in the 1940s. It consisted originally of two pitch-roofed rectangles, one offset from the other but gable end on to the road, with the entrance at

Fig 5.24
Brentwood meeting house by the Lidbetter partnership (1957) with the French doors of the added classroom providing a false entrance.

the intersection of the two. The ancillary rooms were largely in the small front block with the meeting room at the back in the larger block. The simplicity of this design, as well as the main entrance, was subsequently obscured by an extra classroom added at the side with its half-hipped roof and its misleading French doors. A corridor from the main entrance links the classrooms and the meeting room (Fig 5.24).

In contrast, in 1953 Hubert Lidbetter had designed for Watford, a meeting which had been gathering since 1903 in a temporary iron building, a symmetrical and 'modernist' version of his Sutton Coldfield design. A square two-storey meeting room was fronted by single-storey blocks, two side pavilions flanking a recessed lobby block, the whole in brick with flat roofs (Fig 5.25). In the course of time this has acquired numerous accretions including extra storeys and the inevitable pitched roofs. However, the meeting room has retained its original form with wood-block floor and two levels of windows in three bays separated by brick pilasters.

Fig 5.25
Hubert Lidbetter at his most modernist – Watford meeting house as originally built in 1953.

Fig 5.26
*Chelmsford meeting house of
1957/8 by Paul Mauger.*

An interesting comparison is given by the two meeting houses which Paul Mauger designed in the same two counties. His design for the meeting house at Chelmsford built in 1957/8 is along the same lines as Watford or Sutton Coldfield, although on a larger scale. A two-storey square meeting room, this time lit by clerestory windows and with a pyramidal roof, is fronted by a number of single-storey blocks of slightly varying heights. The central block is of five bays, and is plastered, in contrast to the projecting brick pavilions on either side; the bays are delineated by pilasters. To one side another block, containing classrooms and a library, extends backwards alongside the meeting room, just as at Sutton Coldfield (Fig 5.26). The meeting room itself has a wood-block floor, and walls which are wood-panelled above panel heaters. On one side sliding doors give access to a chair store which can increase the floor space, as well providing extra sound insulation from the classrooms beside it. Although thoroughly modernist in approach, the overall design provides a number of pointers to older meeting houses – the pyramidal roof from Earls Colne and the pilasters suggesting the colonnades and

Fig 5.27
*Hitchin meeting house
of 1957. A more highly
decorated building by Paul
Mauger sits in the burial
ground surrounded by
gravestones.*

porticos which were a feature of 19th-century meeting houses – which must have served to make it seem less outlandish.

The old meeting house at Chelmsford had been sold to the local authority and the same fate met the 1838 meeting house (by Samuel Daukes) at Hitchin, Hertfordshire. Friends decided to rebuild on the burial ground in use since 1757, which was on the other side of the Bedford Road from the old meeting house. The design was required to minimise disturbance to the graves and Paul Mauger's fairly conventional design is placed on a concrete raft which is raised a full storey's height above the ground on concrete columns which themselves are resting on piles driven into the ground. The building has two rectangular pitch-roofed blocks at right angles to each other, a double height one for the meeting room and a larger single-storey one for the ancillary accommodation. The walls are of yellow brick with painted concrete panels lining the side walls of the lower range; both ranges have copper-clad roofs. At ground-floor level there is a small glazed lobby area containing the concrete stair which leads to the upper floor (Fig 5.27). The main meeting room is lit by large windows at either end and has plain plastered walls above a timber-panelled dado. The building was given a Civic Trust Design Award in 1962.

Mauger won another Civic Trust award in the same year for his meeting house at Bromley, opened in that year, which echoes some of his earlier designs. This combined a square double-height meeting room at the rear, with clerestory windows and a copper-clad pitched roof, with an L-shaped flat-roofed single-storey block containing lobby and classrooms towards the front of the site.

Although Mauger and Lidbetter could incorporate modernist features into their designs, the Arts & Crafts influence on meeting house design had not yet disappeared. Hubert Lidbetter, in designing a replacement for the bomb-damaged meeting house at Croydon in 1956, clearly had to acknowledge the style of Curtis Green's Adult School Hall, its near neighbour. He combined the low-eaved pantiled roof of the Hall with

Fig 5.28
Croydon meeting house of 1956 by Hubert Lidbetter, echoing the Arts & Crafts style of the next-door Adult School Hall.

the large mullioned and transomed windows he had used at Harrow as the basic components for the block containing the meeting room, adding a gabled three-storey cross wing in a more severe style to contain the ancillary rooms. Dormer windows, of which there are several, project under flat roofs, and the highest window in each gable has a shallow arched head. A portico supported by two cylindrical columns leads to the two double entrance doors which give onto a large lobby area separating the double-height square meeting room from the rest of the building (Fig 5.28).

In the same year, a more thoroughly Arts & Crafts design was built to replace another bomb-damaged meeting house in Canterbury: this was by J L Denman, architect to the Dean and Chapter. Again there are two components, the rectangular meeting house under a hipped roof on the left with arched sash windows, and the more domestic building for ancillary accommodation on the right under a complex roof with hipped dormers, bow windows, casements and leaded lights. The off-set deep-arched porch belongs in style to the latter block and leads into a small lobby from which the meeting room can be accessed (Fig 5.29).

Perhaps the most distinctive of the meeting houses built in the 1950s is that at Weston-super-Mare, whose architect is unknown. It is in a modern Classical style faced in Bath stone, rising to a projecting cornice with plain parapet and hipped roof, and is of rectangular plan with a canted end on the street which contains tall windows comprising glass blocks, so reminiscent of this period. On one side, away from the street, are five modern plain glass windows; on the other is a single-storey side block with an entrance and a canted end lit again by glass block windows, but otherwise blind. It is definitely of its period, but not at all suggestive of a place of worship (Fig 5.30).

All the post-war meeting rooms we have seen so far have been either rectangular or square on plan, the latter perhaps more suitable for worship with a central focus. However, other plan forms were tried out. At Stevenage, Quaker architect William Barnes designed an octagonal

Fig 5.29
The more domestic Arts &
Crafts design of Canterbury
meeting house by J L
Denman, of 1956.

Fig 5.30
Weston-super-Mare meeting
house, opened in 1953, in
a 'stripped-back' Georgian
style reminiscent of municipal
buildings of the period.

meeting room for a meeting house opened in 1959. Originally this
consisted of a single-storey flat-roofed range parallel with the street,
containing ancillary rooms with the meeting room rising behind it. This
latter had a copper-clad shallow roof rising to a lamp finial and was lit by
strip windows just below the eaves. The meeting room, with laminated
wood trusses and plastered walls and ceiling, remains essentially
unchanged, while the other block has been altered, now wrapping round
the meeting room on three sides (Fig 5.31).

Wanstead meeting house was built in 1967 on a burial ground which
had been in use since 1881. The novel but entirely functional design by
Norman Frith consisted of four linked hexagons built in white industrial
brick with monopitch roofs. The two nearest the road are linked by a
glazed lobby behind which rises the larger hexagon which holds the
meeting room. To one side and to the rear, a fourth hexagon contains the
warden's accommodation. The meeting house has full-height windows
occupying half of the three walls which overlook the burial ground and a
complex hexagonal roof structure (Fig 5.32).

Fig 5.31
Stevenage meeting house,
with its octagonal meeting
room as originally built,
photographed in 1959.

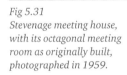

Fig 5.32
Wanstead meeting house of
1968 by Norman Frith.

Both octagonal and hexagonal meeting rooms have proved effective and there are notable examples of each – octagons at Reigate (1984 by Barber, Bundy and partners) and at Devizes (1994 by William Barnes again) – and a further hexagonal design by Normal Frith at Maidstone (1976).

A plan that has only been attempted once is the oval, which James Selby Clewer, architect of the Bournville Village Trust, designed for Redditch Quakers. In the Matchborough area of the new town, a Quaker Housing Association built a development of flats for single persons and single parents, and the meeting house was built on an adjacent plot and opened in 1974. The ancillary rooms, together with various facilities for the tenants, are provided in a single-storey flat-roofed block which surrounds the meeting room, which rises above it. It has windows at clerestory level and a flat green copper roof which is drawn down over the sides to form a decorative fascia (Fig 5.33).

Although the housing development has been a success and has been extended, the meeting itself did not survive into the 21st century and the meeting room has been leased for other purposes. Friends in the area now worship at the contemporary meeting house in Barnt Green, six miles north in the rural outer commuter belt of Birmingham. This meeting was founded in the early 20th century and met in a prefabricated 'tin tabernacle' until the present building was opened in 1969.

Fig 5.33
Redditch meeting house
of 1974 with its oval-plan
meeting room.

Fig 5.34
The interior of the meeting room at Barnt Green.

Fig 5.35
The interior of the meeting room at Chesterfield of 1972, showing a glazed corner block and the lantern atop the pyramidal roof.

The building is another variant on the two-block structure and designed by Edward Jolley Associates. The two square blocks are slightly offset about a lobby area and the whole is of brick, with windows set in panelling interrupting the walls. The block containing ancillary rooms has a flat roof, but the meeting house has a hyperbolic paraboloid roof with glazing at clerestory level. From inside, this roof, lined with tongue and groove panelling, provides a visually interesting contrast in the otherwise plain meeting room (Fig 5.34).

Another 20th-century trend in meeting house design is exemplified here: it is not the shape of the meeting room which gives architectural interest but the form of the roof. A striking instance was the meeting house at Nottingham, designed by Bartlett & Gray in 1961, in which a square meeting room was surmounted by a laminated timber dome of elliptical paraboloid form, with glazing in the curved sides providing top light. This gained a RIBA local award in 1963, but within 20 years there were problems with the structure which had eventually to be replaced by a more orthodox square roof above a clerestory in 2006/7.

Another design by the same architects was provided for Chesterfield in 1971/2 in which a basically square meeting room with chamfered corners produced an octagon with long sides as blank walls and short sides filled by glazing. The whole was covered with a pyramidal roof, lined inside with timber, topped with a lantern (Fig 5.35).

Finally, at Bolton in 1972, W T Gunson & Son designed another square meeting room, this time set on the diagonal with respect both to the road and to the block containing the ancillary rooms. It had a simple monopitch roof, but with its highest point towards the street sloping along the diagonal to the rear, giving room for clerestory windows.

Two notable modernist meeting houses

Of all the meeting house designs of this period, the two which have been most singled out for their architecture are those at Heswall on the Wirral in Cheshire and at Blackheath in greater London. Although they have both been rightly praised for their ingenuity in dealing with difficult sites and their striking external appearance, neither can be said to have been wholly satisfactory at the level of function, being multi-level buildings which do not fit well with the accessibility agenda of the late 20th century.

The meeting at Heswall was founded by a married couple from Birkenhead Quaker meeting in 1937 and met in various hired halls and in Friends' homes until the decision was made in 1958 to build a new meeting house. The site bought later that year on the main street was somewhat cramped and contained a sandstone outcrop. Dewi-Prys Thomas of Beech & Thomas of Liverpool was appointed as the architect and designed a building of two two-storey blocks joined by a short bridge at first-floor level. The left-hand block contained accommodation for resident friends, while the larger right-hand block contained a first-floor meeting room with ancillary facilities on both floors. They were set on the diagonal to the main street on this corner site; the materials were concrete bricks and felted roofs. The building opened in 1962 (Fig 5.36).

Fig 5.36
Heswall meeting house from the road, with the bridge between the two blocks on the left.

Fig 5.37
The interior of the meeting room at Heswall looking towards the windows.

The use of glass is notable: the ground floor lobby is glazed and the meeting room over it has vertical slit windows which increase in height towards the front corner. To one side on the ground floor is an oriel window with tinted yellow glass. This forms part of the internal path to the meeting room which leaves the lobby by a gentle slope past the oriel, turns a corner to face a long stair between blank walls before turning again at the top to enter the meeting room. This was originally part of a much more 'ingenious and highly sophisticated approach', as Pevsner notes,[6] which led the visitor under the bridge between the blocks and round the rear of the building to enter the foyer, evoking the path of the pilgrim from the secular to the sacred, a poetic but not a particularly Quaker idea.

One of the first practical changes to be made was to make an entrance to the meeting house lobby under the bridge. Other prosaic changes which have made the building easier to use are a stair lift and the movement of the kitchen to a small space at the top of the stairs next to the meeting room.

Despite these practical problems, Heswall meeting house is, particularly from the street, a notably successful example of modernist design, softened as it is by the silver birch trees which have been allowed to grow on the rocky ground in front of the building. The meeting room itself is a light airy space well designed for worship (Fig 5.37). The building is carefully finished with mahogany woodwork, fitted window seating in the foyer and specially designed metal chairs in the meeting room.

The architectural importance of Blackheath meeting house was recognised by its listing at Grade II in 2019, one of the very few listed 20th-century meeting houses and the only one from the post-war period. It has been described as 'a small concrete Brutalist jewel',[7] an apparently contradictory statement, but one readily borne out by the view from the south, with the square glazed lantern sitting like a diamond on top of the shuttered concrete walls of the meeting room (Fig 5.38).

Blackheath meeting had its origins in meetings in Deptford and Woolwich which date from the 17th century and which had met in an

Fig 5.38
Blackheath meeting house
from the south showing
the entrance on the upper
floor and the exterior of the
concrete-encased meeting
room with central lantern.
One of the turrets is facing
forwards.

Fig 5.39
Blackheath meeting house
from the south-east at the
lower level with the former
Congregational church hall
on the right.

Fig 5.40
The interior of the meeting
room at Blackheath showing
the central lantern and the
extra light from the concealed
windows at the corners.

adult school hall in Woolwich since 1912. The decision was made to move to Blackheath, where from 1964 Friends met in the hall adjoining the Congregational church. A small piece of land adjacent to the hall became available in 1966 on which to build a meeting house, and Trevor Dannatt, who had recently adapted and rebuilt the church after war damage, was suggested as architect. He had also just prepared designs for the Assembly Hall at the Quaker Bootham School in York with the Quaker engineer Ted Happold of Ove Arup, and this was the team that designed and built the meeting house, which opened in 1972.

The original plan had been for the building to link with the Congregational church hall and for some facilities to be shared. The church and hall were on a lower level, whereas the main entrance for the meeting house was to be on a parallel road which climbed upwards (Fig 5.39). This part of the plan came to naught when the church was closed following the formation of the United Reformed Church in 1974. In addition, parking provision was specified by the local authority, which had to be at the lower level and placed under the building, which was thus part raised on concrete columns.

The main block, which contains the meeting room, is of reinforced concrete with a shuttered surface; the roofs are metal clad. The plan is a square with chamfered corners with the walls at the corners rising to form turrets which conceal top lights. The pyramidal roof rises to a large glazed central lantern. Inside, the meeting room is largely top lit, although there are two slit windows, one of which allows the entrance to be seen; the roof is internally boarded with redwood (Fig 5.40). It has been said to evoke, on a smaller scale, a medieval chapter house, although a closer Quaker comparison would be the second Quaker Friars meeting house at Bristol. A similar plan for the meeting room – champfered corners and a central lantern – was employed in the contemporary meeting house at Chesterfield.

This main block is wrapped round and linked to the Victorian Gothic Congregational hall by a flat-roofed structure in stock brick. This is on two floors, with the upper floor containing a large lobby area, a kitchen and a small WC linked by a staircase with disorientingly angled steps to the lower level with further WCs, a small kitchen and a classroom which can be divided in two by a folding timber screen.

Here, as at Heswall, the meeting room itself is well designed, light but with little in the way of visual distraction. The ancillary spaces would have undoubtedly been differently arranged had there been no need for a link with the church. However, the ingenious use of a small and difficult site is undoubtedly well done and the building, viewed from both levels, a striking one.

Towards and beyond the millennium

Meeting houses continued to be built in small numbers through the last quarter of the 20th century and into the 21st. Few of these were particularly distinguished buildings. They largely continued the themes we have seen so far – single-storey buildings, mainly square meeting rooms, top lit or with windows designed to look out towards garden areas, and well separated from their ancillary spaces. There was also

Fig 5.41
Leeds Carlton Hill meeting
house of 1987.

much adapting of earlier meeting houses to meet modern requirements for disabled access and energy efficiency, for instance: pitched roofs came to replace flat roofs on a number of modernist buildings. It became increasingly important to have spaces to let within premises in order to support Quaker social concerns, to act as a community resource and, with declining membership, to gain income for meetings.

When Quakers in central Leeds finally abandoned the schoolroom of their 1868 meeting house, already owned for the most part by the BBC, they moved a little further up the road and built the new Carlton Hill meeting house adjacent to a social housing scheme. Although a number of prominent architectural practices were consulted, the meeting chose local Quaker architect, Michael Sykes. His design provided not only a meeting room and lettable accommodation for community groups, but an office suite on two floors for the use of a charity, initially Age Concern. There was also accommodation for a caretaker/warden.

Fig 5.42
The 1964 meeting house at
Sheffield by the Lidbetter
partnership, now in
commercial use.

The building, which was opened in 1987, contains a rectangular meeting room under a hipped roof nested into a larger block on two storeys, with a complex roof shape containing a number of dormers. It is built of red brick and tile with yellow brick used as decorative courses, for instance around the gables. Entry is through a porch on the diagonal at one corner of the building which leads into a small lobby (Fig 5.41).

Michael Sykes was also the architect for the current Central Sheffield meeting house, completed in 1990. Friends in Sheffield had been faced with redevelopment of their post-war meeting house – one of the last designs of the Lidbetter partnership, erected in 1964 (Fig 5.42). This latter was an impressive building in brick on a stone plinth with stone dressings, essentially a two-storey block separated into two parts by a lobby issuing from an entrance in the centre of the long side; there was an additional entrance in the end wall. To the north of the central entrance was a four-bay double-height meeting room designed for 250, with a stepped loft over the entrance lobby and large vertical 12-paned windows. To the south, the ancillary facilities were provided on two floors: a flat for the caretaker/warden was built on the flat roof, as it had been at Friends House. It was a structure which could have been built for any number of purposes at any time since the 1930s and was on a scale which one suspects did not fit the times and may have been costly to maintain. Ironically, although the developer completed purchase of the building, it was not in the end demolished and remains in commercial use.

The 1990 meeting house was built on a much smaller scale on a corner plot which slopes down away from St James Street. It is in brick with sandstone dressings with a stone plinth to the rear basement floor and is in a confidently post-modern style. The plan is basically L shaped on three floors with a mezzanine. Each element of the L, where exposed to the street, ends in a prominent gable with arched detailing and canted sides containing windows which, on the first floor at the front, are oriels. A small paved forecourt sits in the angle of the L, with the recessed

Fig 5.43
The current Central Sheffield meeting house, built 1990 to a design by Michael Sykes.

entrance framed by red steel columns, above which is the wall of the first-floor balcony. Inside is a small lobby with stairs and a lift to the other floors. This gives onto a wider lobby which separates the meeting room at the front from the library at the back. The meeting room is essentially a square with canted corners and is well proportioned and lit; it is entered through a double-doored draught lobby, which also provides good sound insulation. The first and basement floors provide most of the ancillary rooms, including a small meeting room (Fig 5.43).

From the 1990s onwards, following a decision not to move the offices of the Society out of London, Friends House has been under an almost continuous programme to fit it internally for the 21st century. From the outside it has remained substantially untouched, although the garden has been redesigned and level access achieved. Inside, however, there is little which has not changed, although the entrance lobby and the stairs at the east end, together with the library reading room, are essentially as they were in 1925. In 2015 the Large Meeting House, now renamed 'The Light', was refurbished by John McAslan & Partners with a design which won a RIBA local award that year. To make it more flexible for letting, moveable banks of stepped seating were installed and these were continued by permanent stepped seating which extended into the former galleries. The meeting house was accessed on the ground floor through vomitoria from the existing cloisters, allowing the original panelling to remain in place. Other original features, such as the ironwork, were also retained.

Fig 5.44
The large meeting house at Friends House, as adapted by John McAslan & Partners, with its stepped pyramidal roof and skylight, and now known as 'The Light'.

Fig 5.45
The interior of Chestnut Hill meeting house, Philadelphia, showing the Quaker Space skyspace by James Turrell, closed but illuminated.

The suspended ceiling was removed and replaced by a pyramidal stepped ceiling of perforated white aluminium, concealing the ventilation and heating systems, with an oblong skylight (Fig 5.44).

This latter was a nod to the Skyspace designs of the American Quaker artist, James Turrell, who is much concerned in his art with the interplay of light and space. Skyspaces are buildings containing an oblong aperture which can be opened to the sky. Looking calmly upward through the aperture produces a meditative experience and, particularly when the sky is changing, allows the viewer to confront the construction of reality.

Turrell has collaborated with two Quaker meetings and their architects in the US to produce meeting houses which contain such structures – Live Oak meeting house, Houston (2001), and Chestnut Hill Friends Meeting, Philadelphia (2013) (Fig 5.45), but no British meeting house has yet taken up the challenge, although there are permanent skyspaces at the Kielder Water & Forest Park (Cat cairn, 2000) and the Yorkshire Sculpture Park (Deer shelter, 2007).

Since the 2011 commitment to sustainability, Quakers have been more than ever insistent that their meeting houses should act as a public witness to that testimony. The three most recent meeting houses to be built demonstrate that commitment in interestingly different ways.

After many years of discussion, Quakers in Kingston-upon-Thames sold their 18th-century meeting house on a main shopping street and moved in 2014 to a site surrounded by a park, just beyond the inner ring

Fig 5.46
Kingston-upon-Thames
meeting house, showing the
interior circulation space
illuminated by the central
light well.

Fig 5.47
The interior of the meeting
room at Kingston-upon-
Thames showing the central
lantern and the concealed
lights at the corners.

road. Here John Langley of Tectus Architecture designed a multipurpose building, a single-storey mainly flat-roofed pavilion on a nearly square plan with a perimeter colonnade of regularly spaced grey steel piers, the path paved with hand-made red bricks. The walls are of stock brick, interrupted where appropriate with full-height glazing panels.

The entrance leads into a hall running the length of the building: to the right are the classrooms and committee rooms and to the left, the meeting room, a second smaller hall and a kitchen. A glass-enclosed courtyard, open to the sky, lies between the hallway and the meeting room (Fig 5.46). The meeting room itself is square with wooden panels on two walls and windows to the courtyard and garden, the rest being plastered. Light comes from the windows, from cut-aways in the corners of the roof, and from a central small square lantern at the apex of a shallow pyramidal roof, both features which reference the Blackheath design (Fig 5.47).

Energy efficiency and sustainability are central to the structure. The building is heated by air-source heat pumps in conjunction with underfloor heating and cooling. Raised zinc-clad air-cooling stacks are a significant feature on the roof. In 2015, the building was the joint winner of the ACE/RIBA award for religious architecture.

Stockport Quakers had a fairly plain flat-roofed prefabricated meeting house of 1979 in two blocks separated by a lobby, which was by the 2010s costing too much to be sustainable. On the same site they erected in 2015 a building designed by the Bernard Taylor Partnership, who had recently refurbished the ancillary spaces at Mount Street, Manchester. This is in red brick on an L plan, the two blocks each having a monopitch roof, the two sloping away from each other (Fig 5.48). The central entrance has a glazed and aluminium-framed porch. The block to the right contains the main meeting room, a rectangular space with suspended ceiling with a nine-light horizontal window on the long wall and a five-light window to the front. The roof of this block carries two rows of photovoltaic panels. The block to the left of the entrance contains the lobby and the ancillary rooms. Compared with Kingston, this is a more orthodox design, but again

Fig 5.48
Stockport meeting house
(2015).

Fig 5.49
Hammersmith meeting house
(2020) – the exterior from
the garden.

Fig 5.50
Hammersmith meeting house
– the circular double-height
meeting room with lighting
largely through the clerestory.

it has been built with sustainability in mind, having extensive insulation in walls, floor and roof as well as triple-glazed windows.

Friends in Hammersmith have worshipped since 1955 in a Hubert Lidbetter-designed meeting house which had a meeting room based on the earlier war-damaged building even to the extent, at this late date, of having a ministers' stand. It was surrounded on three sides by ancillary facilities in single-storey flat-roofed blocks. This has been under threat of redevelopment for some time, with a new site offered not far away. For this site, hemmed in by Victorian terraced housing, the architect, Stuart Dodd has designed a double-height circular wood-panelled meeting room lit largely by clerestory windows, wrapped round on two sides by ancillary rooms, the whole linked by a reception area from which all rooms can be accessed. The building, which opened in 2020, is built to 'Passivhaus' standards, which ensure very little energy is needed for space heating and cooling. Only ethical supply chains have been used to source all materials (Figs 5.49 and 5.50).

On reflection

The design of Quaker meeting houses from the 17th through to the 19th century contained a discernible thread of function which dictated a simple rectangular auditorium space with at one end the ministers' stand. The move via a transitional evangelistic model of worship in the mission halls to the renewed expectation that all Friends had the potential to offer ministry severed that functional thread and changed the design of meeting houses.

Other denominations underwent similar changes during the 20th century, with an increasing concentration on the importance of the laity, a group unknown among Quakers, but the continuing centrality of preaching and/or the eucharist within these denominations meant that the thread of function was maintained. Nevertheless, a willingness to play with alternative forms for churches and chapels, including octagons, squares and circles, can be seen in the buildings of other denominations. It could be said that in the later 20th century Quaker meeting houses found themselves, perhaps for the first time, part of a broader development in religious architecture.

Perhaps the future may show the establishment of a new functional thread which will anchor meeting house design. But for now, it is best to see the 20th and 21st centuries as times of change and experimentation.

Notes

1   Church rates were levied by the parish vestry on all parishioners for the upkeep of the church and were, like tithes, resisted by many Nonconformists, but especially by Quakers.
2   Now occupied by the British Medical Association.
3   Endsleigh Gardens occupied an area to the south of Euston Road between Gordon Street and Woburn Place; it was bordered on the south by the street with the same name – historically it was the southern half of Euston Square Gardens.
4   *Architectural Review*, October 1927 as quoted in the list entry for Friends House at historicengland.org.uk/listing/the-list/list-entry/1078321.
5   Six Weeks Meeting is a meeting of London Friends first set up in 1671 to act as a 'court of appeal and advice' when George Fox set off to visit America that year. It very soon took over all property matters for all meetings in London and Middlesex. It was superseded in 2017 by the London Quakers Property Trust.
6   Pevsner and Hubbard 1971, 237.
7   Quaker Meeting Houses Project Report at heritage.quaker.org.uk/files/Blackheath LM.pdf.

6 Quaker architecture

The development of the meeting house

In religious architecture, as in other fields, there is an expectation that form will in general follow function. However, other influences are detectable, such as tradition, artistic fashion, the emergence of new building techniques and the use of structures to express theological ideas. So the general form of Christian churches arose from that of the basilica, the major Roman public building, with its apsidal end and its nave and aisles. The cruciform shape came later in the development of church architecture and embodied the major theological symbol of the cross in the shape of the building. The development and elaboration of the pointed arch through the medieval period largely followed from technical developments in masonry allowing lighter and therefore taller structures to be constructed, reaching up towards the heavens. The use of Gothic or Classical forms for churches in the post-medieval period was largely an expression of artistic fashion linked to a desire to return to a simpler, more rational style rooted in mathematical form (Classical) or to evoke the high point of pre-reformation Catholic practice (Gothic). So when English dissenters came to build Gothic churches in the 19th century, they were not only returning to a form which made more sense of their renewed interest in liturgy, but also implicitly claiming that they were as much the inheritors of the true church as the Anglicans.

However, their predecessors in the 17th century were in the business of breaking with tradition if they thought about the matter at all. Although early dissenting buildings were constructed in a variety of styles as well as the vernacular, building on a rectangular plan soon became standard. It took two forms – the long wall form in which both the entrances and the pulpit were on the long sides of the rectangle (which owed something to Scottish Presbyterian practice) and the gable-end form in which the entrances and pulpit were on the short sides of the rectangle at opposites ends of the worship space. The major functional requirement for these preaching boxes was that the congregation could be able to hear the minister.

Nevertheless, we find Quaker meeting houses taking up both these forms. The similarity of Brigflatts to a long-wall meeting house of the period has already been noted. Norwich Gildencroft adopted both its long-wall plan and its external form from the nearby Old Meeting House (*see* Figure 2.3). Gable-end entry is much rarer in Quaker meeting houses, but we do find it among early modifications to meeting houses, as at Stourbridge and Painswick.

Quakers, however, developed a variant on the long-wall form in which the entrance is on one long side but the ministers' stand, the Quaker equivalent of the pulpit, is on one of the gable ends. This form, which has a number of variants described by Butler, was predominant well into the 19th century. The entrance is usually asymmetrically placed in the first or second bay and leads either straight into the meeting room or into a lobby, often stretching the whole width of the building, not unlike the screens passage in a medieval hall house, with the meeting room entered through central doors in a screen to one side. Swarthmoor and Hertford both have this form and in both cases the passage/lobby has a gallery over it with stairs leading up from the lobby. There can also be ancillary rooms leading out of the passage on the ground floor.

Square plans are much rarer among Quaker meeting houses until the 20th century and, aside from the early example of the hexagonal meeting house at Burlington, New Jersey, no other experiments in plan form were attempted until after Yearly Meeting 1904 had agreed that Friends speaking from all parts of the meeting room should be equally audible.

Galleries[1] are a feature shared with other places of worship of the 18th and 19th centuries as a way of providing extra space for worshippers especially for special occasions. Where they remain in old meeting houses, they can be raked or stepped and almost always are provided with simple forms as seating (*see* Great Yarmouth): this might indicate that only servants or poorer Quakers were expected to use these spaces.

The other additional space which was provided in Quaker meeting houses was a separate room in which a women's business meeting could be held at the same time as the men's business meeting. As explained earlier, this was usually only necessary when the meeting house was one at which monthly or quarterly meetings (for Friends from the local area or from the whole county, respectively) were held. At a local level, business meetings could be held more easily at different times or in different places, perhaps in the meeting house and in a nearby house: women's meetings at Rookhow were apparently held in the caretaker's kitchen in the adjoining cottage.

A women's meeting house could be in a separate building, as at Hertford, or a separate room, as at Wandsworth, but most often it was obtained by dividing off part of the meeting house with removable wooden shutters set into an appropriate frame. This is seen at its simplest at Skipton, where the single-celled meeting house was divided by a screen some 30 years after it had been built. Where a meeting house had been provided with a gallery, the gallery could be shuttered off as the women's meeting room (as at Alton and Stourbridge) or the room under the gallery could serve this purpose (as at Airton and Swarthmoor). In the latter case, the women's meeting room was on the opposite side of the lobby to the main meeting room and so two sets of shutters had to be used to link the two rooms together. It is likely that shutters would have been in place for most of the time and men's and women's meeting rooms only combined for the sort of large occasions for which galleries would be used.

Shutters in early meeting houses could hinge upwards and be attached to the ceiling by hooks, hinge sideways like window shutters, slide in grooved channels like sashes or be entirely removeable. In the larger meeting houses of the late 18th and early 19th centuries, sashed shutters came to dominate and, if counterweighted appropriately, could be moved upwards into the roof space or down into the floor. Winches could also be used.

Since the necessity of having rooms available for two contemporaneous business meetings was restricted to Friends, internal shutters are almost entirely restricted to Quaker meeting houses, although the author knows of at least one Methodist chapel where the gallery can be isolated in this way.

There seems not to have been any need felt for other facilities at a meeting house, other than provision for horses and carriages, before the 19th century. Large urban meeting houses seem to have included toilet facilities initially in separate buildings, only moving indoors after the provision of mains drainage. Men's and women's cloakrooms or retiring rooms are also found at about the same time, for instance at York and Darlington. York also had a strong room for the safe storage of documents, which before might have been kept in a locked chest.

Although schools were early associated with meeting houses, the provision of separate classrooms, as at Pardshaw, seems to have been the exception before the rise of First-day schools and adult schools in the 19th century. The provision of kitchen facilities in meeting houses seems to have been a 20th-century development. The provision of such ancillary facilities as toilets, kitchens, classrooms and committee rooms, both for the meeting itself and for community use, became then one of the major functional requirements for meeting house design.

The furnishing of the meeting room

Quaker worship had since the beginning consisted in expectant waiting for a message to be given through one of the Friends present. Stillness, silence and lack of visual interest are aids to this waiting, but not its essence. Quaker places of worship are thus meeting houses in the plain meaning of the words. The basic functional requirement which they have to fulfil is to be a place for meeting.

The message, when it comes, is nonetheless important. The initial realisation that some Friends were more likely to give ministry than others led to those 'recorded' ministers sitting apart and raised up on the ministers' stand. The strenuous assertion of the discipline in the 18th century led to elders sitting in the fixed bench below or to the side of the stand from which they could effectively regulate the meeting. At some point it seems that overseers joined them and there became a need sometimes for more than two rows of fixed benches.

From the beginning there were two forms of the stand. The shorter form, sometimes described as 'pulpit-like', occupied only the central part of the wall of the meeting room. In its simplest form it is found at Brigflatts, Come-to-Good, Ettington and Wallingford. In some cases it has on a lower level at either side fixed seats for the elders, and in this form it is found at Farfield, Marazion and Uffculme (Spiceland).

What came to be the dominant form, however, was a structure which occupied the whole of the wall of the meeting room and had more than one row of fixed benches at different levels, with the highest level reserved for ministers (and sometimes with a gated entrance, as in many pulpits) with the lower benches used by elders and overseers. This is seen early at Hertford, Jordans and Crawshawbooth, but by the 19th century is effectively ubiquitous.

The walls of meeting houses were almost always covered at the lower level by a wooden dado or wainscot, almost always of vertical planking but occasionally panelled. From what little evidence is available, these were rarely painted before the 20th century; in the 19th century they may well have been stained and varnished. The dado was almost certainly practical since it would have been easier to clean than plaster.

Windows were in general set above the wainscot. When the change to sashes was made to increase light in the meeting room, they tended to be set higher to give the maximum of light with the minimum of visual distraction. This seems particularly the case in large towns and cities. On constricted sites, as we have seen, light could be supplied by clerestories or lanterns. These became in more frequent use in the late 20th century, as life outside the meeting house became potentially more intrusive.

In many meeting houses there are fixed benches attached to some walls but, in general, seating was provided by free-standing wooden forms or benches. These would have been arranged in rows facing the stand, the benches either spanning the whole width of the room, as seen at Farfield and Jordans, or with a central aisle, as seen at Coanwood and Lancaster. Butler suggests that central aisles were a consequence of the arrival of free-standing stoves for heating in the 19th century, which is the case at these latter two meeting houses. The presence of aisles was in any case merely for access, as there is no processing during Quaker meetings, not even at weddings and funerals. Women and men would have sat on different sides of the meeting house as seen in the painting of Gracechurch Street, although which side was allocated to the women would have been according to local custom. In only one meeting house is there a wooden barrier between the two sides and that is at Rawdon near Leeds, where there was a Quaker school, to avoid distraction of the pupils. Others are reported to have existed in similar circumstances.

In the 20th century the move was to the use of chairs rather than benches in meeting rooms, although many old meeting houses retained at least an example of their benches for use. This suited the change to a circular arrangement of seating centred on a table for meeting for worship. Meeting rooms also increasingly became multi-functional spaces, let on other than Sundays for a variety of community purposes.

As has been seen in some of the pictures earlier in this book, in older meeting houses, the change in arrangement leads to an appearance of a modern meeting 'camping out' in a meeting room designed for a completely different form of worship.

The Quaker style

Quakers pretty much take the distinctiveness of Quaker buildings for granted. The typical Quaker view might be conveniently summed up by a quote from Hubert Lidbetter in *The Friends Meeting House* (1961)[2]: 'Meeting Houses … have always been merely useful buildings of the utmost simplicity and appropriateness for their purpose, resulting in truthful building'.

Quaker buildings are distinctive because they are 'of the utmost simplicity'. This simplicity, Lidbetter argues, comes from the expression of a distinctive function which Quaker buildings are called on to perform and also, implied here by the use of 'simplicity' and 'truthful', is that the buildings somehow embody these particular elements of Quaker witness.

David Butler, in *The Quaker Meeting Houses of Britain* (1999), also uses both these explanations. 'Convenience for purpose defines the whole development of Quaker meeting houses', he maintains.[3] Neither George Fox, in the epistles, nor subsequently Yearly Meeting, made any attempt to set out any instructions for the construction of meeting houses. That there is such essential uniformity across the country is, he reasons, because 'they [Friends] observed their testimony to simplicity in all aspects of their lives'. Others have been more direct and claimed that Quaker buildings express an aesthetic of plainness.

The testimony to simplicity or plainness was one of the most vexed issues within Quakerism in the long 18th-century. Scarcely a Yearly Meeting goes by without the epistle exhorting Friends vigorously not to indulge in the latest trends in dress and furniture and to protect their children from the pernicious effects of fashion. Curiously, nothing is ever said about simplicity in buildings, either houses or meeting houses.

Utility was, however, used as a yardstick by Friends, particularly in judging what was appropriate for Quaker children to learn. Therefore, there is no surprise that we can appreciate in many early meeting houses that form is following function in specifying the need for a ministers' stand, for the possibility of a second meeting room for the women's business meeting and for providing porches and lobbies to keep out the worst of the weather. For the rest it is clear that tradition plays a part, in encouraging the use of vernacular styles, in the use of front-facing form or bench seating and in the segregation of the sexes, which was also seen in other places of worship.

In the example of the ministers' stand, we see this being no longer provided in meeting houses from the 1890s onwards, some 30 years before the official recording of ministers was abolished. Most likely abolition was only the last formal act in a process which had been going on for many years. Other changes, such as the the decline in gender-segregated seating in meeting houses; the increasing theological liberalism of British Friends; and the existence of alternative forms of Quaker worship and of ministry may have combined to reduce the status of the minister and therefore the use of the ministers' stand less frequent.

Additional functions became important in the Quaker meeting house over the same time period, as the provision of toilet accommodation; the importance of social facilities, such as kitchens; education for young and old requiring classrooms. These changes made floor space for ancillary accommodation more important and, because the noise from such activities was potentially disruptive of worship, led to the segregation of these functions from the meeting room itself, hence the ubiquity of the multiple-block model of meeting house design in the 20th century.

I feel it is relatively straightforward to see that Quaker meeting houses constitute a building type, distinct from that of other religious buildings, for, at least before the 20th century, they contain unique features not found elsewhere. However, the issue of whether there is a Quaker style of religious architecture is a much more open question.

The characteristics which have frequently been recognised as 'Quaker' – plainness, simplicity, sobriety – were, as Emma Lapsansky has pointed out, rarely closely defined and their limits clearly changed with time.[4] Friends, when exhorting others to faithfulness in these matters, were for the most part warning against the following of worldly fashion and the conspicuous consumption that went with it, leading to vanity and the measuring of human worth in material rather than spiritual terms. They were certainly not in the business of defining a Quaker aesthetic or insisting on uniformity in design – that would have been a 'silly poor gospel' in Margaret Fell Fox's memorable phrase.[5]

Certainly, early meeting houses in the vernacular style seem to us in the modern day to be the epitome of simple fitness for purpose, which might well justify Lidbetter's pronouncement above. Yet even here, as for instance in the turned balusters of the ministers' stand at Farfield, decoration is not shunned and quality of workmanship is respected. And, as we have seen in Chapter 2, Quakers were building at the same time in Bristol and Norwich meeting houses which were every bit as up-to-date and aesthetically pleasing as those of other dissenters.

The relative uniformity of the interior arrangements in meeting houses is surely a witness to Quakers being aware of what other Quakers were building. But in the case of Norwich Gildencroft, we also have a pretty obvious case of Quakers not only being aware of the buildings of others, but using them as models.

It is also clear that Quakers have built meeting houses in many of the architectural styles available to them, including Classical and Gothic, Arts & Crafts and modernism, and it is not surprising that they should have done, particularly since they began to use professional architects to design meeting houses. What becomes obvious from examination of these buildings is that, for the most part, they are of the plainest and least decorated form of the style. In Classical buildings, columns are usually of the Doric or Tuscan orders with undecorated capitals and largely plain entablatures: only Manchester Mount Street, with its strong Greek Revival influence, has an Ionic portico. Similarly, the few Gothic meeting houses lack tracery in the windows, while there is no sign of the pinnacles which decorate even such a restrained Gothic chapel as Charles Barry's Upper Brook Street chapel in Manchester.

In common with what we know of Quaker dress, Quaker architecture also tended in the past to adopt recognised styles only when they were no longer in the forefront of architectural fashion. This may apply less to the last century or so when my impression is that Friends were in general more adventurous, both the neo-Georgian style of Friends House and the brutalism of Blackheath being pretty much on trend for the mid-1920s and the mid-1970s, respectively. However, neither of these styles became very popular for meeting houses and those styles which did, such as a vague Arts & Crafts style as well as watered-down modernism, seem to have been used for longer among Friends.

In summary, the lack of any centralised planning, together with a general indifference to the importance of buildings, has meant that Quaker meeting houses are largely diverse in appearance. Until late in the 19th century, a uniformity in the functional requirements for Quaker worship meant that the interior design of meeting houses was largely conserved, while the strength of the national community of Friends meant that one or two overall meeting house designs became fairly common. Nevertheless, there were always sufficient meeting houses with a distinctive style of their own to prevent the identification of a uniform 'Quaker style'.

However, there does seem to be a sense of integrity, if not of simplicity, in Quaker buildings of the first two centuries to distinguish them from other religious architecture and to support the assertion of a unique building form.

The transformation of the Society in the 20th century and, in particular, the growth in the number of 'convinced' as against 'birthright' Friends has weakened this sense of national community and led to a rise in the importance of the local worshipping group. This, together with the change in the functional constraints on worship, has acted to increase the diversity of Quaker buildings and made the search for the elements of a Quaker style even more elusive. This may, as I have suggested, just be the mark of a transitional period in British Quaker architecture, but it makes it difficult to affirm now the assurance of earlier writers that simplicity and truthfulness are necessarily embodied in the Quaker meeting house.

Notes

1   Throughout this book I have used 'gallery' to mean a structure which provides seating on an upper level for occasional use. In Quaker usage it was sometimes, confusingly, used to describe the ministers' stand and those reading further in the literature may wish to note this. The use of the term 'ministers' stand' also almost completely died out in the 20th century and most Quakers would now refer to the structure as the 'elders' bench', which indicates its last remembered use. The responsible elder in a particular meeting now tends to sit somewhere on the inner row of chairs.

2   Lidbetter 1961, 5.

3   Butler 1999a, 888.

4   Lapsansky 2013.

5   From a manuscript in the Library of the Society of Friends (Portfolio 25/66), written in 1700.

Bibliography

Primary source

This book was initially conceived as an outcome of the Quaker Meeting Houses Heritage Project. This, as described in the Preface, was a national survey of Quaker meeting houses which covered those properties still being used as meeting houses and those still owned by Quaker meetings, but not used specifically as meeting houses. As such, the primary sources for the information in the book are the reports compiled for each meeting house surveyed together with the National Overview Report, which are all available online at heritage.quaker.org.uk.

Secondary sources

No student of Quaker meeting houses can get far without reference to the work of David Butler and of Christopher Stell. Butler is comprehensive and includes all known meeting houses up until and including the 1990s: Stell is more selective and is best on pre-19th-century examples. They are as follows:

Butler, David M 1978 *Quaker Meeting Houses of the Lake Counties.* London: Friends Historical Society

Butler, David M 1999a *Quaker Meeting Houses of Britain*. 2 volumes. London: Friends Historical Society

Stell, Christopher 1986 *An Inventory of Nonconformist Chapels and Meeting-Houses in Central England*, RCHME. London: HMSO

Stell, Christopher 1991 *An Inventory of Nonconformist Chapels and Meeting-Houses in South-West England*, RCHME. London: HMSO

Stell, Christopher 1994 *An Inventory of Nonconformist Chapels and Meeting-Houses in the North of England*, RCHME. London: HMSO

Stell, Christopher 2002 *An Inventory of Nonconformist Chapels and Meeting-Houses in Eastern England*. Swindon: English Heritage

Other sources

Alexander, William 1820 *Observations on the Construction and Fitting up of Meeting-houses &c. for public worship…* York: William Alexander

Anon 1918 'An Irishman at London Yearly Meeting in 1794'. *Journal of the Friends Historical Society* **15** (1), 4

Arnold, H Godwin 1960 'Early Meeting Houses'. *Transactions of the Ancient Monuments Society* **8**, 89

Barter, Marion, Greenhow, Ingrid, and Monckton, Linda 2016 'Quaker Meeting Houses in Britain' in Historic Churches. Tisbury: Cathedral Communications

Beck, William, and Ball, T Frederick 1869 *The London Friends' Meetings*. London: F Bowyer Kitto (facsim reprint London: Pronoun Press 2009)

Butler, David M 1967 'Meeting Houses Built and Meetings Settled'. *Journal of the Friends Historical Society* **51** (3), 174–8

Butler, David M 1999b 'Untolerated Meeting Houses'. *Journal of the Friends Historical Society* **58** (3), 207–19

Clark, Joanna 2006 *Eminently Quakerly*. London: Quakerbooks

Cooksey, Pamela (ed) 2011 *The Large and Small Notebooks of Joseph Wood: A Yorkshire Quaker (1750–1821); A Transcription*. Huddersfield: Society of Friends

Gawne, Eleanor 1998 'Buildings of Endearing Simplicity: The Friends Meeting Houses of Hubert Lidbetter'. *Twentieth Century Architecture* **3**, 86–92

Hinshaw, Seth Beeson 2001 *The Evolution of Quaker Meeting Houses in North America 1670–2000*. M.Sc. thesis, University of Pennsylvania. https://repository.upenn. edu/cgi/viewcontent.cgi?article=1373&context=hp_theses. Accessed 30 August 2020

James, William 1902 *The Varieties of Religious Experience*. London: Longmans, Green & Co

Lapsansky, Emma J 2013 'Plainness and Simplicity' *in* Angell, Stephen W, and Dandelion, Pink (eds) *The Oxford Handbook of Quaker Studies*. Oxford: Clarendon Press

Lidbetter, Hubert 1961 *The Friends Meeting House*. York: William Sessions (2nd edn 1979)

Martin, Christopher 2009 *A Glimpse of Heaven*. London: English Heritage

Nickalls, John L (ed) 1952 *The Journal of George Fox: A Revised Edition*. Cambridge: Cambridge University Press (a more modern edition by Nigel Smith was published in Penguin Classics in 1998 but is long out of print)

Penney, Norman 1907 'The First Publishers of Truth'. *Journal of the Friends Historical Society*, Supplements 1–5

Pevsner, Nikolaus, and Hubbard, Edward 1971 *The Buildings of England: Cheshire*. Harmondsworth: Penguin Books

Radice, Paula 2016 *Quakers in Hastings: The Making of a Community, 1673–1920*. Hastings: Religious Society of Friends

Roethe, Johanna 2019 '"Of Singular Elegance and Dignified Simplicity": Quaker Meeting Houses and their Architects' *in* Aldrich, Megan, and Buchanan, Alexandrina (eds) *Thomas Rickman and the Victorians*. London: Victorian Society

Southall, Kenneth H 1974 *Our Quaker Heritage*. London: Quaker Home Service (second impression 1984)

Tanner, William 1858 *Three Lectures on the Early History of the Society of Friends in Bristol and Somersetshire*. London: Alfred Bennett

Watts, Michael R 1978 *The Dissenters I: From the Reformation to the French Revolution*. Oxford: Clarendon Press

Watts, Michael R 1995 *The Dissenters II: The Expansion of Evangelical Nonconformity*. Oxford: Clarendon Press

Watts, Michael R 2015 *The Dissenters III: The Crisis and Conscience of Nonconformity*. Oxford: Clarendon Press

Wakeling, Christopher 2017 *Chapels of England: Buildings of Protestant Nonconformity*. Swindon: Historic England

Wilson, Stephen 1975 'From Devonshire House to Endsleigh Gardens'. *Journal of the Friends Historical Society* **53** (4), 293–313

Glossary of architectural terms

Styles of architecture

Arts & Crafts	The Arts & Crafts movement was initiated in reaction against the perceived impoverishment of the decorative arts under the influence of industrialisation and stood for traditional craftsmanship.
Classical	Architecture which is more or less consciously derived from the principles of Greek and Roman architecture of classical antiquity.
Doric	The oldest (dating to the 6th century BCE) and plainest of the three basic orders of classical Greek architecture. A Doric column is stout, with a fluted shaft (ideally, with 20 flutes), a plain capital and no base.
Gothic	Architecture of the high or late medieval period characterised by pointed or ogee arches – the reference to the Goths was originally pejorative – the style probably derives from Arab models.
Ionic	The second oldest (mid-6th to 5th centuries BCE) of the three basic orders of classical Greek architecture. An Ionic column is tall and slender, with a fluted shaft of 24 flutes, a capital with prominent volute scrolls and an elegantly moulded base.
modernism	In architecture was associated with an analytical approach to the function of buildings, a strictly rational use of (often new) materials, structural innovation and the elimination of ornament.
Tuscan	In ancient Rome, the Doric order was often replaced with the 'Tuscan' order indigenous to the Italian peninsula; it consisted of an unfluted shaft, a simply moulded capital and a base.
vernacular	Architecture created from mostly local materials, by and for the use of local people.

Building materials

ashlar	Masonry made of large square-cut stones usually laid in courses.
cob	A material made from subsoil, water, fibrous organic material (typically straw) and sometimes lime.
quoin	A large, prominent masonry unit outlining windows, doorways, segments and corners of buildings.
render	A coat of plaster applied to a brick or stone surface.
roughcast	Plaster of lime, cement and gravel, used on outside walls.

rubble	Masonry of rough, uneven building stone set in mortar, but not laid in regular courses.
stucco	A form of render which contains aggregate, forming a rougher outer surface.

Building elements

architrave	The lintel or beam that rests on the capitals of columns. The term can also apply to all sides, including the vertical members, of a frame with mouldings around a door or window.
baluster	A vertical supporting element, similar to a small column.
balustrade	A railing supported by balusters.
bay	A section of a building distinguished by vertical elements such as columns or pillars; a section of a building containing an opening, eg a door or window.
blind	Refers to sections of a building that might contain a window or a door but where there is only plain masonry.
buttress	A structure of stone or brick built against a wall to strengthen or support it.
chamfer	A symmetrical sloping surface at an edge or corner.
colonnade	A range of columns that supports a string of continuous arches or a horizontal entablature.
corbel	A structural piece of wood, stone or metal protruding from a building to carry the weight of an element above, eg an overhanging roof.
cornice	Any horizontal decorative moulding that crowns a building element – strictly the topmost part of an entablature.
dado	The lower part of a, usually internal, wall below the dado rail.
entablature	The structure of mouldings and bands which lies above columns on a Classical building, sometimes divided into architrave, frieze and cornice.
lintel	The horizontal block that spans an opening between two supports, also called an architrave.
ogee	Element, such as an arch or moulding, that is S-shaped.
pediment	The usually triangular element in a Classical gable above the lintel or entablature.
pilaster	A shallow, non-structural rectangular column, attached to, and projecting only slightly from, a wall surface.
portico	A porch leading to the entrance of a building, sometimes extended as a colonnade.
vomitorium	A passage situated below or behind a tier of seats, as in a Roman amphitheatre or modern football stadium.

Window elements

casement	A window frame that is hinged on one vertical side, and which swings open to either the inside or the outside of the building.
clerestory	A high section of wall that contains windows above eye level, originally the topmost level of windows in the nave of a church.
dormer	A perpendicular window located in a sloping roof; triangular walls join the window to the roof.
lantern	Originally an openwork timber construction placed on top of a building to admit light and allow smoke to escape, now more usually of stone or metal and glazed.
mullion	The vertical element that forms a division between units of a window.
oriel	A projecting window typically of an upper floor, supported from below by a bracket.
sill (or cill)	The horizontal surface at the bottom of a window.
transom	The horizontal element that forms a division between units of a window – in the US also refers to a window set above a door, what in the UK is known as a fanlight.

Roof forms

eaves	The projecting edge of a roof that overhangs an exterior wall to protect it from the rain.
gable	A roof with two slopes – front and rear – joining at a single ridge line parallel to the entrance façade. When the ridge line of a gable-roofed house is perpendicular to the street, the roof is said to be a 'gable-end roof".
hipped roof	A roof with four sloped sides.
mansard	A four-sided hipped roof featuring two slopes on each side, the lower slopes being very steep, almost vertical, and the upper slopes sometimes being so horizontal that they are not visible from the ground.
monopitch roof	A single-sloped roof surface, often not attached to another *roof* surface. Can be referred to as a pent or lean-to roof.
pitched roof	A roof that slopes downwards, typically in two parts at an angle from a central ridge.

Glossary of Quaker terms

Basic vocabulary

concern	The spiritual conviction of an individual Friend to perform a particular witness or other action, which they are obliged to bring before other Friends for testing before they act on it. If approved by a business meeting the concern is said to be 'adopted' by the meeting, who will both support the Friend concerned and join with them in the action.
discernment	The process used by Friends for distinguishing right understandings of spiritual experience from mistaken ones based on the individual and corporate experience of the group; plays a leading part in the communal testing of concern.
Friend	This is the term Quakers use of themselves and in their official title, the Religious Society of Friends.
Light	One of the main terms Friends use for the unmediated experience of God, which is central to their theology; usually referred to as 'the Inward Light' or 'the Light Within' and sometimes identified by early Friends as 'the Light of Christ'.
membership	Until the mid-18th century there was no formal membership of the Society of Friends, it being felt that joining in worship with Friends and the appearance of a changed life and witness sufficiently indicated a person as a Friend. The process of becoming a Friend was described as convincement. Meetings were scrupulous in declaring publicly that persons whose lives did not reflect well on their apparent association with Friends were not in fact 'in unity with them'.
	After the institution of formal membership in the late 18th century, membership could be acquired in two ways, by birthright or by convincement, which involved being visited by Friends appointed by the meeting. Formal rules were also introduced for 'disowning' Friends whose behaviour fell short in various ways, most notable of which were payment of tithes, marriage before a priest and failure in business.
ministry	A spoken contribution in a meeting for worship.
Quaker	This name for a member of the Religious Society of Friends is a nickname given to George Fox and his early followers by a justice of the peace in Derby in 1650 because 'we bid them tremble at the word of God'.
testimony	The outward manifestation of experience of the Light in a Friend's life – also called 'witness'; some elements of testimony which have been tested over the years can be considered, particularly in recent times, as corporate testimonies of the Society, eg equality, simplicity, sustainability and peace.

Truth	Another of the terms used of the Inward Light, sometimes expressed as the 'Spirit of Truth'.
witness	The outward manifestation of experience of the Light in a Friend's life – also called 'testimony'.
worship	Quaker worship consists in an expectant waiting for a message to be given by one of those present; silence is a helpful but not necessary prerequisite for such worship.

Organisation

Meeting	This term is used both for a gathering of Friends and for the worshipping community in a particular place or area.
Meeting for business	A meeting for worship in which the business of the worshipping group is transacted and in which the concerns of individual Friends are tested.
Meeting for worship	A gathering of Friends for worship.
Men's meeting	The business meeting open to the men of a worshipping group (usually a monthly meeting) which dealt largely with property and finance as well as concern for the wellbeing and behaviour of men friends.
Monthly meeting	Both the group of Friends in a particular area consisting of a number of worshipping groups and the meeting for business of that group, held monthly (in the 21st century renamed an Area Meeting).
Quarterly meeting	Both the group of Friends in a particular county and the meeting for business of that group, held quarterly (no longer in the 21st century a regular part of Quaker organisation).
Women's meeting	The business meeting open to the women of a worshipping group (usually a monthly meeting) which dealt largely with charity as well as concern for the wellbeing and behaviour of women friends and children. The existence of women's meetings led to provision of separate spaces for the women to meet for business.
Yearly meeting	Both the national organisation of Friends in a country and the annual meeting for business, which is the ultimate constitutional authority of a national group of Friends, as Britain Yearly Meeting. Confusingly, the geographical scope of a yearly meeting can encompass less than a whole country. In former times also used for a meeting, held yearly, at which Friends from a number of counties met, eg the Yearly Meeting for the Northern Counties.

Roles

clerk

The clerk of a meeting for business is responsible for the conduct of the meeting and most significantly for drafting the minutes, which are presented and agreed in the meeting. They have in the past been responsible also for keeping the meeting's records (of membership, including births, marriages and deaths).

elder

Elders in Quaker meetings are responsible for the right holding of meetings for worship and for providing educational opportunities within meetings. They were originally those Friends with the longest experience of Quakerism – the so-called 'antient friends' – later appointments, which continue to this day, to recognise Friends with appropriate experience and practice in discernment.

minister (or recorded minister)

Quakers, as radical exponents of 'the priesthood of all believers', have never had a trained and paid ministry. However, it was early recognised that some Friends had a greater gift for spoken ministry in meeting for worship. These Friends were identified by their local meetings and because they were often freed to travel and to minister to other congregations, where they would be given hospitality, the decision was made to record them centrally in the 1730s. In the UK the practice was discontinued in 1924.

overseer

Overseers in Quaker meetings are responsible for the pastoral care of the worshipping community. The term is probably derived from the overseers of the poor, who were responsible in parishes for collecting for the poor and disbursing charity.

Buildings and their furniture

adult school

Building for educational activities, usually on a Sunday, for the working class.

book cupboards

Book cupboards were a feature of meeting houses in which to keep the meeting house library of approved Quaker books for loan. These books were supplied centrally from London, at an agreed price, to all meetings.

elder's bench

A 20th- and 21st-century usage for the stand, since after the recording of ministers ceased, elders continued to sit on these benches.

facing bench(es)

Another word for the stand, so-called because all the other seats in a meeting house would have originally faced the stand.

gallery

In this book, a raised area of seating at the back or sides of a meeting house and used for occasions when large numbers of seats were required. These also feature in chapels and churches of other denominations in the 18th and 19th centuries. Confusingly the term is used at some times and in some places for the stand.

Institute	Building for social and educational activities for Quakers, largely for unmarried men.
meeting house	The building or room in which meeting for worship takes place.
screen	Screens with moveable sections are a frequent feature of meeting houses and enabled either the separation of the space to allow separate men's and women's business meetings to take place at the same time or the opening up of the space to allow large numbers of Friends to be accommodated for special occasions.
	Early screens had sections which could be physically removed or were hinged or slid like sashes. Larger meeting houses had screens which constituted a whole wall and complex systems were developed with winches or counterweights so that they could disappear upwards into the ceiling or down below into the floor.
seating	Meeting houses have from the first contained seating for the worshippers. These would originally have been forms – flat boards with no backs. These developed into benches by the addition of backs, originally at right angles, eventually swept back for extra comfort (the width of the seat being increased at the same time). Many meeting houses have fixed benches against some of the walls; the others would have been free-standing and facing the stand. Access could be from the sides or there would be a central aisle. Commercially supplied benches did not become usual until the 19th century. Chairs or a mixture of benches and chairs are most commonly found in the meeting houses of today.
	Until late in the 19th century, men and women would have been seated separately on either side of the meeting house.
stand (or ministers' stand)	The structure at one end of a meeting house which contains at least one bench seat raised above the floor level, usually with a rail, balustrade or panel in front of it. There is typically sufficient space between the bench and the rail for a Friend to kneel in prayer. The stand can occupy only a part of the wall on which it is placed or the whole of it and can have up to four tiers of benches. Ministers were expected to sit at the highest level with other officers of the meeting (elders and overseers) at lower levels. Access steps are typically provided at either end of the raised bench(es) or in the middle.

Gazetteer of listed Quaker buildings

The buildings listed below are given, within each listing grade, in date order, earliest built first. The full listing details can be found online at historicengland.org.uk/listing/the-list/ or at britishlistedbuildings.co.uk.

Quaker buildings are not routinely open to the public but can welcome visitors by appointment. Contacts and times of meetings for worship are available at www.quaker.org.uk/meetings.

Grade I

Building	Date	Notes	Architect	Address	Postcode	Grid reference
Hertford FMH	1670			50 Railway Street, Hertford	SG14 1BA	TL 32812 12705
Brigflatts FMH	1675			Brigflatts, Sedbergh	LA10 5HN	SD 64089 91155
Ifield FMH	1675/6			7 Langley Lane, Ifield, Crawley	RH11 0NB	TQ 25244 37910
Jordans FMH	1688			Welders Lane, Jordans, Beaconsfield	HP9 2SN	SU 97454 91022
Brant Broughton FMH	1701			3 Meeting House Lane, Brant Broughton	LN5 0SH	SK 91653 54217
Come-to-Good FMH	1710			near Feock (Helford Passage), Truro	TR3 6QS	SW 81278 40325
Quakers Friars	1747–9	b, c	George Tully	The Friary Building, Quakers Friars, Bristol	BS31 3DF	ST 59275 73318

Grade II* (Grade B in Scotland and Grade 2 in Wales)

Building	Date	Notes	Architect	Address	Postcode	Grid reference
Swarthmoor Hall	late 16th century	a		Swarthmoor Hall Lane, Ulverston	LA12 0JQ	SD 28186 77293
Blue Idol FMH	c 1580	a		Oldhouse Lane, Coolham	RH13 8QP	TQ 10739 23125
Amersham FMH	c 1600	a		Whielden Street, Amersham	HP7 0JB	SU 95609 97044
Almeley Wootton FMH	1672			Almeley Wootton	HR3 6PX	SO 33276 52425
Alton FMH	1672			39 Church Street, Alton	GU34 2DA	SU 71728 39689
Cirencester FMH	1673			53 Thomas Street, Cirencester	GL7 2BA	SP 02079 02243
Adderbury FMH	1675	b		Horn Hill Road, West Adderbury	OX17 3EW	SP 46515 35300
Cartmel Height former FMH [Barrow Wife]	1677	b,c		Barrow Wife, Height Road, Cartmel Fell	LA11 6NZ	SD 40682 84824
Settle FMH	1678			Kirkgate, Settle	BD24 9DX	SD 81819 63663
Ettington FMH	1684–9			Halford Road, Ettington	CV37 7TH	SP 26772 48701

Building	Date	Notes	Architect	Address	Postcode	Grid reference
Swarthmoor FMH	1688			Meeting House Lane, Ulverston	LA12 9ND	SD 28378 76875
Marazion FMH	1688/9			Beacon Road, Marazion	TR17 0HF	SW 51849 30701
Colthouse FMH	1688/9			Colthouse, Near Hawkshead	LA22 0JU	SD 35887 98174
Farfield FMH	1689	b, c		Bolton Road, Addingham	LS29 0RQ	SE 07610 51790
Nailsworth FMH	1689			1 Quakers Close, Chestnut Hill	GL6 0RA	ST 84793 99520
Stourbridge FMH	1689			37 Scotts Road, Stourbridge	DY8 1UR	SO 89908 84525
Airton FMH	from 1690s	a		Airton	BD23 4AE	SD 90307 59215
Yealand FMH	1692			18 Yealand Road, Yealand Conyers	LA5 9SH	SD 50384 74425
Warwick FMH	1695			39 High Street, Warwick	CV34 4AX	SP 28071 64737
Dolobran FMH	1700	d		Dolobran Isaf, Pont Robert, Meifod	SY22 6HU	SJ 12370 12419
Lancaster FMH	1708			Meeting House Lane, Lancaster	LA1 1TX	SD 47298 61681
Burford FMH	1708/9			Pytts Lane, Burford	OX18 4SJ	SP 25241 12093
Crawshawbooth FMH	1716 and 1736			13 Co-operation Street, Crawshawbooth	BB4 8AG	SD 81079 25366
The Pales FMH	1716 and 1745	d		near Llandegley, Llandrindod Wells	LD1 5UH	SO 13798 64058
Long Sutton FMH	1717			Langport Road, Long Sutton	TA10 9NE	ST 46710 25923
Wallingford FMH	1724			13 Castle Street, Wallingford	OX10 8DL	SU 60702 89627
Rookhow FMH	1725	b		Rusland, Ulverston	LA12 8LA	SD 33223 89542
Claverham FMH	1729			Meeting House Lane, Claverham	BS49 4PB	ST 45262 66285
Pardshaw FMH	1729			Pardshaw, Cockermouth	CA13 0SP	NY 10378 25463
Stafford FMH	1730			Foregate Street, Stafford	ST16 2PX	SJ 92017 23719
Coanwood FMH	1760	b, c		Coanwood, near Haltwhistle	NE49 0PU	NY 70993 58940
North Walsham FMH	1772			Quakers Hill, Mundesley Road, Swafield	NR28 0RF	TG 28516 31732
Brentford & Isleworth FMH	1785			Quakers Lane, London Road, Isleworth	TW7 5AZ	TQ 16349 76881
Spiceland FMH	1815			Uffculme, Cullompton	EX15 3AZ	ST 08315 14055
Kendal FMH	1816		Francis Webster	Stramongate, Kendal	LA9 4BH	SD 51778 92808
Malton FMH	1823	d		Greengate, Malton	YO17 7EN	SE 78729 71890

Building	Date	Notes	Architect	Address	Postcode	Grid reference
Norwich FMH	1826		J T Patience	Upper Goat Lane, Norwich	NR2 1EW	TG 22802 08656
Darlington FMH	1839/40		Joseph Sparkes	6 Skinnergate, Darlington	DL3 7NB	NZ 28702 14395
Ackworth FMH	1847	c	J P Pritchett	Barnsley Road, Ackworth, Pontefract	WF7 7LT	SE 44147 17281
St Andrews FMH	1860s	a, d	John Chesser	2 Howard Place, St Andrews	KY16 9HL	NO 50548 16750
Central Edinburgh FMH	1865	a	Paterson and Shiells	7 Victoria Terrace, Edinburgh	EH1 2JL	NT 25557 73514
Dundee FMH	1891		Malcolm Stark and Rowntree	7 Whitehall Crescent, Dundee	DD1 4AR	NO 40345 30124
Friends' Institute Building	1897	a, b, c	Ewan and James Harper	220 Moseley Road, Birmingham	B12 0DG	SP 08086 85316
Kelso FMH	19th century	a, d		12 Abbey Row, Kelso	TD5 7JF	NT 72884 33973

Grade II (Grade C in Scotland) – only included if referenced in book

Building	Date	Notes	Architect	Address	Postcode	Grid reference
Broad Campden FMH	possibly c 1500	a		Meeting House Lane, Broad Campden	GL55 6US	SP 15819 37941
St Helens FMH	late 16th century	a		Church Street, St Helens	WA10 1AJ	SJ 51477 95251
Portishead FMH	probably c 1670	a		11 St Marys Road, Portishead	BS20 6QP	ST 46572 75517
Faringdon FMH	1672			4, Lechlade Road, Faringdon	SN7 8AQ	SU 28533 95590
Skipton FMH	1693			The Ginnel, Newmarket Street, Skipton	BD23 2JA	SD 99120 51543
Rawdon FMH	1697			Quakers Lane, Rawdon	LS19 6HU	SE 20796 40063
Huntingdon FMH	17th century	a		48a Post Street, Godmanchester	PE29 2AQ	TL 24441 70734
Penrith FMH	17th century			Meeting House Lane, Penrith	CA11 7TR	NY 51643 30404
Bridport FMH	probably late 17th century			95 South Street, Bridport	DT6 3NZ	SY 46624 92577
Worcester FMH	1701			Sansome Place, Worcester	WR1 1UG	SO 85012 55221
Askwith former FMH [Quaker Cottage]	1704	b,c		Back Lane, Askwith	L21 2JA	SE 17032 47929

Painswick FMH	1705/6			Vicarage Lane, Painswick	GL6 6XS	SO 86988 09742
Frandley School Room	1726	a,b		Sandiway Lane, Antrobus, Northwich	CW9 6LD	SJ 63614 79234
Earls Colne FMH	c 1733			4 Burrows Road, Earls Colne	CO6 2RZ	TL 85639 29009
Disley FMH	1740	a		Ring O'Bells Lane, Disley	SK12 2AG	SJ 97535 84436
High Flatts FMH	1754/5			9 Quaker Bottom, High Flatts	HD8 8XU	SE 21232 07461
Kings Lynn FMH	early–mid 18th century	a		38 Bridge Street, Kings Lynn	PE30 5AB	TF 61881 19560
Gildersome FMH	1756			75 Street Lane, Gildersome	LS27 7HX	SE 24332 29076
Winchester FMH	c 1773	a		16 Colebrook Street, Winchester	SO23 9LH	SU 48489 29182
Sawley FMH [now private residence]	1777	b		Sawley Road, Grindleton	BB7 4RS	SD 77268 46688
Wandsworth FMH	1778			59 Wandsworth High Street, London	SW18 2PT	TQ 25725 74618
Winchmore Hill FMH	1790		John Bevans	59 Church Hill, Winchmore Hill, London	N21 1LE	TQ 31295 94657
Pickering FMH	1793			19 Castlegate, Pickering	YO18 7AX	SE 79795 84336
Ross-on-Wye FMH	1805			3a Brampton Street, Ross-on-Wye	HR9 7EQ	SO 60101 24489
Great Yarmouth FMH	1807			17 Howard Street South, Great Yarmouth	NR30 1LN	TG 52330 07546
Frenchay FMH	1809			Beckspool Road, Frenchay	BS16 1NT	ST 64118 77884
Milford Haven FMH	1811		Griffith Watkins	Priory Road, Milford Haven	SA73 2DT	SM 90368 06081
Uxbridge FMH	1817			York Road, Uxbridge	UB8 1QW	TQ 05663 84326
Warrington FMH	1830			1b Academy Place, Warrington	WA1 2NR	SJ 60772 88208
Central Manchester FMH	1831		Richard Lane	6 Mount Street, Manchester	M2 5NS	SJ 83780 97991
Gloucester FMH	1834/5		Samuel Daukes	Greyfriars, Southgate Street, Gloucester	GL1 1TS	SO 83077 18364
Reading FMH	1835			2 Church Street, Reading	RG1 2SB	SU 71744 73017
Littlehampton FMH	c 1835	a		23 Church Street, Littlehampton	BN17 5EL	TQ 03032 02147
Wellington FMH	c 1845		Francis Fox	High Street, Wellington	TA21 8RA	ST 13994 20660
Street FMH	1850		J Francis Cotterell	36 High Street, Street	BA16 0EB	ST 48502 36935
Wisbech FMH	1854		Algernon Peckover	21 North Brink, Wisbech	PE13 1JR	TF 45822 09625

Cartmel FMH	1859		Alfred Waterhouse	Haggs Lane, Cartmel, Grange-Over-Sands	LA11 6PH	SD 38244 78556
Salisbury FMH	mid-19th century	a		51 Wilton Road, Salisbury	SP2 7EP	SU 13572 30393
Old Broadcasting House	1868	b, c	Edward Birchall	148 Woodhouse Lane, Leeds	LS2 9EN	SE 29826 34467
Frandley FMH	1881			Sandiway Lane, Antrobus, Northwich	CW9 6LD	SJ 63614 79234
Birkenhead FMH	1892		G E Grayson	83 Park Road South, Birkenhead	CH43 4UU	SJ 30706 88644
Edgbaston FMH	1893		William Henman	St James Road, Edgbaston	B15 1JP	SP 05803 85746
Bournville FMH	1905		W A Harvey	65 Linden Road, Birmingham	B30 1JT	SP 04456 81405
Hampstead FMH	1907		Fred Rowntree	120 Heath Street, London	NW3 1DR	TQ 26396 86084
Letchworth FMH	c 1907		Bennett & Bidwell	Howgills, 42 South View, Letchworth	SG6 3JJ	TL 21903 31945
Adult School Hall	1908	a, b	W Curtis Green	60 Park Lane, Croydon	CR0 1JE	TQ 32545 65178
Golders Green FMH	1913		Fred Rowntree	17 North Square, Hampstead Garden Suburb, London	NW11 7AD	TQ 25503 88563
Friends House	1925/7		Hubert Lidbetter	173–177 Euston Road, London	NW1 2BJ	TQ 29617 82481
Malvern FMH	1937/8		J R Armstrong	1 Orchard Road, Malvern	WR14 3DA	SO 77742 45594
Croydon FMH	1956		Hubert Lidbetter	60 Park Lane, Croydon	CR0 1JE	TQ 32542 65217
Blackheath FMH	1971/2		Trevor Dannatt	Lawn Terrace, London	SE3 9LL	TQ 39518 75930

Notes
FMH – Friends Meeting House
a – not built as a meeting house
b – no current meeting for worship
c – not owned by Quakers
d – not referenced in this book

Illustration Credits

Every effort has been made to trace the copyright holders and we apologise in advance for any unintentional omissions, which we would be pleased to correct in any subsequent edition of this book.

Illustrations are sourced and reproduced by kind permission as follows:

Source: artist
© Michael Macintosh Fig 1.17

Source: Bristol Museum and Art Gallery, UK/Bridgeman Images
© Bridgeman Images – Fig 2.1 (69790)

Source: Butler (1999a) with permission Fig 4.5

Source: Historic England Archive (application for the reproduction of these images should be made to Historic England Archive)
Fig 1.1 (BB65/00728 and BB65/00726), Fig 5.1 (BL28897/001), Fig 5.4 (BL29057), Fig 5.7 (BL28783), Fig 5.8 (BL28999)
© Historic England Archive Fig 1.3 (DP175649), Fig 1.16 (DP160410), Fig 1.20 (DP033075), Fig 1.21 (DP033076), Fig 2.4 (DP160135), Fig 2.5 (DP160137), Fig 2.9 (DP160125), Fig 2.11 (DP160119), Fig 2.10 (DP160121), Fig 2.17 (DP000760), Fig 2.22 (DP023189), Fig 2.24 (DP160686), Fig 2.25 (DP160690), Fig 3.12 (DP166205), Fig 3.13 (DP166201), Fig 3.14 (DP233781), Fig 3.15 (DP233787), Fig 4.26 (DP158323), Fig 4.27 (DP158324), Fig 4.47 (DP157564 and DP166647), Fig 4.49 (DP150908), Fig 4.50 (DP088253), Fig 4.51 (DP088390), Fig 5.36 (DP143768), Fig 5.38 (DP151456), Fig 5.39 (DP151458)
© David Guthrie Fig 3.3 (IOE01/04164/14)
© Krystyna Szulecka Fig 4.10 (IOE01/12310/08)
© Mr Bob Cottrell Fig 3.6 (IOE01/14654/34)
© Mr Chris Ayre Fig 3.8 (IOE01/01813/34)
© Mr Graham R Heasman Fig 5.21b (IOE01/16401/24)
© Mr Nigel Wood Fig 2.16 (IOE01/10314/11)
© Mr Peter Hyde Fig 3.16 (IOE01/11110/33)
© Mr Robin Earl Fig 5.23 (IOE01/03446/33)
© Mr Stanley J. Russell Fig 1.18 (IOE01/09157/07)
© Mr Terry Abbiss Fig 4.28 (IOE01/11218/14)

Source John Hall Quaker Meeting House Flickr Albums [www.flickr.com/photos/qmh]
© John Cottis Fig 3.1, Fig 3.2
© John Hall Fig 1.4, Fig 1.5, Fig 1.6, Fig 1.7, Fig 1.8, Fig 1.11, Fig 2.6, Fig 2.12, Fig 2.13, Fig 2.15, Fig 2.19, Fig 2.21, Fig 2.23, Fig 2.26, Fig 3.7, Fig 3.9, Fig 3.17, Fig 3.18, Fig 3.21, Fig 3.22, Fig 4.2, Fig 4.4, Fig 4.7, Fig 4.13, Fig 4.14, Fig 4.16, Fig 4.18, Fig 4.21, Fig 4.25, Fig 4.30, Fig 4.34b, Fig 4.35, Fig 4.36, Fig 4.37, Fig 4.40, Fig 4.41, Fig 4.43, Fig 4.46, Fig 5.9, Fig 5.10, Fig 5.11, Fig 5.12, Fig 5.13, Fig 5.15, Fig 5.16, Fig 5.18, Fig 5.19, Fig 5.20, Fig 5.21a, Fig 5.22, Fig 5.24, Fig 5.26, Fig 5.27, Fig 5.28, Fig 5.29, Fig 5.30, Fig 5.32, Fig 5.33, Fig 5.34, Fig 5.35, Fig 5.40, Fig 5.41, Fig 5.43, Fig 5.46, Fig 5.47, Fig 5.49
© Joseph McGarraghy Fig 4.32, 4.34a
© Richard Hoare Fig 5.42

© Wendy Harris Fig 4.15

Source: Library of the Religious Society of Friends
© Britain Yearly Meeting
Fig 3.19 [TEMP MSS 824] (from a copy in the author's possession), Fig 3.20 [PIC/F072]

Source: Lidbetter (1961) with permission
Fig 4.1, Fig 4.3, Fig 4.9, Fig 5.2

Source: photographer
© Andy Vail Fig 4.42
© Bessie White Fig 3.23
© Chris Skidmore Fig 1.9, Fig 1.10, Fig 1.12, Fig 1.13, Fig 1.14, Fig 1.15, Fig 1.22,
    Fig 1.24, Fig 1.25, Fig 1.26, Fig 2.8, Fig 2.14, Fig 2.20, Fig 3.4, Fig 3.10, Fig 3.11,
    Fig 3.24, Fig 3.25, Fig 3.26, Fig 3.28, Fig 3.29, Fig 3.30, Fig 3.5, Fig 4.6, Fig 4.11,
    Fig 4.12, Fig 4.19, Fig 4.20, Fig 4.22, Fig 4.23, Fig 4.24, Fig 4.31, Fig 4.38,
    Fig 4.39, Fig 5.37
the late George Plunkett, with permission Fig 2.3
© Graham Beckley Fig 2.18
© Hufton and Crow Fig 5.44, Fig 5.5
© Julian Osley Fig 1.2
© Matt Davis Fig 4.17, Fig 4.33
© Meg Twycross Fig 0.1, Fig 0.2
© Neil Alexander Downie Fig 5.48
© Peter Blaker Fig 4.29
© Preservation Maryland Fig 2.28
© Ray Kilby Fig 5.50
© Rob Farrow Fig 2.7
© Ron Saari Fig 2.29
© Steve Minor Fig 3.27
© Terry Foss Fig 5.45
© W David Wallace Fig 2.30

Source: Quaker meetings
Bournville Meeting archive, with permission Fig 4.44, Fig 4.45
© Malvern Quaker Meeting Fig 5.14
Preston Patrick Quaker meeting, with permission Fig 1.23
Sibford Quaker meeting, with permission Fig 1.19
© Watford Meeting archive Fig 5.25

Source: Quaker & Special Collections, Haverford College, Haverford, PA
Fig 2.27 (US Friends Meeting Houses [HC.MC.912])

Source: RIBA pix
© Architectural Press Archive/RIBA Collections Fig 5.3, Fig 5.6, Fig 5.17

Source: Rijksmuseum Fig 2.2

Source: Stevenage Museum
© G L Blake Fig 5.31

Index

Entries for common features of meeting houses refer in general to discussions of the particular feature: descriptions of its form in particular meeting houses are found under the entry for the meeting house.

Page numbers in *italics* refer to illustrations and in **bold** refer to tables.